The series
„Sustainable Peace and Global Security Governance"
is edited by

Bonn International Center for Conversion (BICC) GmbH
and
Geneva Centre for the Democratic Control of Armed
Forces (DCAF)

Volume 1

Roland Friedrich | Arnold Luethold (eds.)

Entry-Points to Palestinian Security Sector Reform

Nomos

The Geneva Centre for the Democratic Control of Armed Forces (DCAF) publishes studies, reports, and books on security sector governance worthy of public consideration. The views and opinions expressed (unless otherwise declared) are those of the authors and do not necessarily reflect those of DCAF, its sponsors, or its editors.

Die Deutsche Nationalbibliothek lists this publication in the Deutsche Nationalbibliografie; detailed bibliographic data is available in the Internet at http://www.d-nb.de .

ISBN 978-3-8329-3530-6 (Nomos Verlag, Baden-Baden)
ISBN 978-92-9222-061-7 (DCAF, Geneva)

Original Versions:
English and Arabic, Geneva and Ramallah, 2007

Contents

Acronyms

DCAF	Geneva Centre for the Democratic Control of Armed Forces
DCO	District Coordination Office
DDR	Disarmament, Demobilisation and Reintegration
DFLP	Democratic Front for the Liberation of Palestine
DIA	Defence Intelligence Agency
DGIS	Director-General of Internal Security
DGPS	Director-General of Preventive Security EU European Union
EUCOPPS	European Union Coordination Office for Palestinian Police Support
GI	General Intelligence HCNS Higher Council of National Security
IDF	Israel Defence Forces
IED	Improvised Explosive Device
ISF	Internal Security Forces
ITAG	International Transition Assistance Group
IUED	Institut Universitaire d'Etudes du Développement / Graduate Institute for Development Studies (Geneva)
JD	Jordanian Dinar
JSC	Joint Security Committee
NAD	Negotiation Affairs Department (PLO)
NGO	Non-Governmental Organisation
NSC	National Security Council
NSF	National Security Forces
OG	Official Gazette
PCPSR	Palestinian Center for Policy Survey and Research
PFLP	Popular Front for the Liberation of Palestine
PICCR	Palestinian Independent Commission for Citizens' Rights
PLC	Palestinian Legislative Council
PLA	Palestine Liberation Army
PLO	Palestine Liberation Organisation
PNA	Palestinian National Authority
PRCs	Popular Resistance Committees
RPG	Rocket-Propelled Grenade
RSC	Regional Security Committee
SAI	Strategic Assessments Initiative
SSR	Security Sector Reform
TRCT	Treatment and Rehabilitation Center for Victims of Torture
TSPT	Transitional Security Planning Team
UK	United Kingdom
UN	United Nations
US	United States
USD	US Dollar
USSC	United States Security Coordinator

Introduction

Roland Friedrich and Arnold Luethold

The first *Oslo Agreement* of 1994 established the Palestinian National Authority (PNA) and provided for a system of limited self-governance in the Palestinian Territories. Ever since, security has been at the centre of Palestinian-Israeli relations: Security was a key issue in all Israeli-Palestinian agreements concluded during the interim period up to 1999; then, during the second *Intifada*, security became a cornerstone of all internationally-sponsored diplomatic initiatives and peace plans and, subsequently, of public discourse.

Palestinian security sector reform (SSR) has only very recently begun. The very fault lines, perceptions and interests, which have characterised the Israeli-Palestinian conflict, also shape the debate on security sector reform. Thus, 'security sector reform' carries different meanings for different actors: For a majority of Palestinians, SSR is about the development of a fully-fledged functional security sector, which protects them against Israeli incursions and provides the basis for statehood and sovereignty. Israel, in turn, looks at Palestinian SSR as a means for enhancing her own security; accordingly, Israel expects SSR to produce a system of Palestinian policing, too weak to constitute a danger and strong enough to confront the "infrastructure of terror". The US, several European and some Arab states, very much in line with Israel, see SSR essentially as a process to revive the system of policing laid out in the *Oslo Agreements*. Finally, some other countries emphasise the importance of good governance: for them, only a well-governed security sector can be effective; the challenge of SSR, according to this view, lies in building security organisations, which function in a transparent manner and are fully accountable to the elected executive and legislative authorities.

Depending on their interests, various countries have sought to influence Palestinian SSR, both conceptually and practically, in different directions and a variable degree of transparency. Some dispatched assistance missions to the Palestinian Territories, and an increasing group of international experts are delivering technical aid to selected Palestinian security personnel. What has been missing most so far is a genuinely Palestinian perspective on the current SSR process and its direction, achievements and challenges. The present volume aims to address this shortfall. It combines a number of chapters by Palestinian security experts, researchers and practitioners, which address various aspects of security sector reform in the Palestinian Territories.

As all the contributions were written before June 2007, this book does not specifically discuss the problems that have been created as a result of the armed conflict between Hamas and Fatah, which ended with Hamas' seizure of control of the Gaza strip on 15 June. Nor does it cover changes in donor behaviour since. However, it would be wrong to conclude from this that the book has become outdated. On the contrary, the events in Gaza and the subsequent political difficulties cannot be understood without being placed and analysed within the wider context of security sector governance and its structural problems, of which they are a reflection. So, in many ways the various contributions, which look at the underlying structural problems, should also help the reader better understand events that have occurred since June 2007.

The contributions in this book have largely relied on primary sources and firsthand information, which are difficult to access for outsiders and non-Arabic speakers. The volume pursues two main objectives: firstly, it seeks to provide local perspectives on security sector governance and highlight entry-points for reform. Secondly, the book aims to give a voice to the intended beneficiaries of security sector reform, namely the Palestinians. By doing so, the publication hopes to contribute to a better understanding of Palestinian security needs and the direction in which Palestinians would like to see their security sector evolve. International assistance to security sector reform in the Palestinian Territories, if it seeks to promote stability in the longer term, may need a much better understanding of both.[1]

Concepts and Definitions

Readers may find the concepts and terminology in the rapidly growing literature on security sector governance confusing. This is not surprising, as key terms and concepts are often used with different meanings.

Security Sector Governance

The term 'security sector', for instance, is associated with many competing definitions, which include either a narrow or a broad set of actors. In the very narrow sense, 'security sector' refers only to state organisations authorised to use force. On the other side, the United Nations Development Programme (UNDP) suggested in its Human Development Report of 2002 a broad definition that also includes civil management oversight bodies, justice and law enforcement institutions, non-statutory security forces and civil society groups.[2]

A governance and development perspective is more lenient to the broader definition.[3] In the Palestinian context, where non-statutory actors play an important role and where a state formation process is under way, a too narrow definition of the security sector would fail to understand the forces that shape it. Thus, this publication uses the term 'security sector' in the very broad sense. Accordingly, the Palestinian security sector comprises at least five categories of actors:

1. *Organisations authorised to use force*: Internal Security Forces (Civil Police, Preventive Security, Civil Defence, Executive Force[4]), National Security Forces (including Naval Police, Military Police, Military Intelligence and Military Liaison), Presidential Security/Force 17, Presidential Guard, General Intelligence;
2. *Civil management and oversight bodies*: President, Prime Minister, National Security Council, Palestinian Legislative Council and select committees, Ministries of the Interior, Foreign Affairs and Planning, customary and traditional authorities, financial management authorities (Ministry of Finance, Bureau of Financial and

Administrative Control), Palestinian Independent Commission for Citizens Rights' (PICCR);

3. *Justice and law enforcement institutions*: Regular courts (Magistrate Courts, Courts of First Instance, Courts of Appeal, High Court), High Constitutional Court, High Criminal Court, administrative courts, *Shari'a* and religious courts, military courts, High Judicial Council, Ministry of Justice, Correction and Rehabilitation Centres, Criminal Investigation Departments, Public Prosecution, customary and traditional justice systems;

4. *Non-statutory security forces*: *Izz ad-Din al-Qassam Brigades* (military wing of Hamas), *Al-Aqsa Martyrs Brigades* (Fatah affiliated armed groups), *Al-Quds Battalions* (military wing of Islamic Jihad), *Nasser Salah ad-Din Brigades* (military wing of the Popular Resistance Committees), *Martyr Abu Ali Mustafa Battalions* (military wing of the Popular Front for the Liberation of Palestine, PFLP), *National Resistance Brigades* (military wing of the Democratic Front for the Liberation of Palestine, DFLP);

5. *Non-statutory civil-society groups*: professional groups (such as Palestinian Bar Union, Palestine General Federation of Trade Unions, Palestinian Federation of Industries, Union of Palestinian Medical Relief Committees), media (such as *Al-Quds* newspaper, *Al-Ayyam* newspaper, *Maan* News Agency, *Ramattan* Studios), research organisations (such as Applied Research Institute Jerusalem (ARIJ), *Bisan* Center for Research and Development, Palestinian Academy for the Study of International Affairs (PASSIA), Palestinian Center for Policy and Survey Research (PCPSR), Palestinian Council on Foreign Relations (PCFR)), advocacy organisations (such as *Al-Haq* – Law in the Service of Man, *Addameer* Prisoners Support and Human Rights Association, *Mandela* Institute for Political Prisoners, *Al-Mezan* Center for Human Rights, Palestinian Center for Human Rights (PCHR)), religious organisations (such as Higher Islamic Council, *Zakat* Centers, religious charitable organisations), other non-governmental organisations (such as community development centres and women, enviromental, and health NGOs), universities (such as *Birzeit* University, *Al-Quds* University, *An-Najah* University, Islamic University Gaza, *Al-Azhar* University Gaza).[5]

In the specific case of the Palestinian Territories, one may also wish to add the Occupying Power, Israel, and her security sector as a sixth category of *external actors*. To the extent that the separation lines between Palestinian and international security actors have become blurred, it might be useful to include in this category also the US and other state actors involved in equipping and training some of the Palestinian security forces.

Security Sector Governance

The term *'security sector governance'* implies that security is no longer the exclusive realm of *government* or state actors; it involves several categories of non-state actors. From a normative viewpoint, the concept of 'security sector governance' establishes a link between the *security sector* and *good governance*. Transparency, accountability and participation are considered basic requirements of good governance. Thus, the underlying assumption is that a well-governed security sector requires more than just well trained and equipped security forces. It requires *transparency* of the decision-making in security matters; it also requires a *framework of accountability* under which security forces and government are accountable to the people and/or their elected representatives; and it requires broad-based support for the policies pursued, hence *inclusiveness* of all categories of security sector actors. From a more descriptive viewpoint, 'security sector governance' describes the organisational structures, systems and processes that security sector actors, both public and private, use for coordinating their interests and making and implementing policy decisions.

This volume is concerned only with security sector governance in the Palestinian Territories. It does not include Palestinian security mechanisms and actors in the Diaspora, such as the armed elements of the Palestine Liberation Organisation (PLO) and other factions that exist or have existed in countries such Algeria, Egypt, Iraq, Jordan, Lebanon, Sudan, Syria and Yemen.

Security Sector Reform

Ongoing military occupation and four years of intensified violence and armed conflict have shattered the Palestinian security infrastructure. Palestinians face the political and institutional task of establishing a functioning security sector. Depending on the assessment of the stage of development of the Palestinian security sector, this challenge may be described as either *security sector transformation, security sector reconstruction* or *security sector reform*. Common to all these terms is the establishment of a security sector, in which both its operational components and its oversight structure function according to the principles of good governance and provide security and justice to the people.[6] Security sector reform comprises thus many different activities, such as:

- The strengthening of the rule of law and the establishing of a strong legal framework that provides for critical oversight;
- The strengthening of democratic control over security organisations by the executive, the legislature, the judiciary and civil society organisations;
- The development (training and equipment) of professional security forces;
- The development of regional security cooperation;
- Peace-building and demilitarisation (reconciliation, frameworks for peace and economic stability, disbanding armed groups, disarmament, reinsertion of armed combatants into civilian activities).

In the Palestinian Territories, most of these activities also provide *possible entry-points to security sector reform*, or openings to more comprehensive and wider transformation of the sector. However, it is important to note that successful security sector reform requires a broad and coordinated approach, in which the different activities are interlinked, mutually supportive and properly sequenced. In the Palestinian case, over-emphasis on one single set of activities risks being highly counterproductive.

Palestinian Security Sector Governance and SSR

Palestinian security sector governance is highly complex and shaped by domestic, regional and international factors. Internally, it has been in a process of transition since the return of the PLO in 1994. Power struggles between Fatah and Hamas, bitter feuds within Fatah and heightened internal violence have added to this complexity.

Externally, Palestinian security sector reform is constrained by Israeli occupation. Through the presence of its armed forces and settlements, Israel maintains a strong physical presence in East Jerusalem and the West Bank. In the Gaza Strip, Israel has maintained control over entry- and exit-points by land and sea and over the airspace, as well as over the population registry. The increased territorial fragmentation and the limited security, administrative and legislative powers that the PNA has been able to exert over Gaza and some areas in the West Bank have hindered Palestinian security sector reform.

Reconstructing and reforming a security sector in a situation of armed conflict and in the absence of a state framework is a difficult undertaking. In order to familiarise the reader with the intricacies of Palestinian security sector governance in the Palestinian Territories, a brief analytical account of the PNA security sector and its evolution might be of help. Three phases of development can be distinguished here since the inception of the PNA in 1994.

Security Sector Governance and SSR under Arafat (1994-2004)

During the ten years of Yasser Arafat's presidency the PNA had a centralised decision-making system with strong authoritarian and neo-patrimonial traits. In this system, the late Arafat was the unrivalled linchpin; he relied on a combination of political cooptation, financial accommodation and intense micro-management to secure his rule.

A central element of Arafat's power structure was his direct control over the various PNA security organisations which had been created in 1994 and later. Arafat governed the security sector through a strategy of 'divide and rule': he established different organisations with overlapping or parallel functions and fostered competition between their commanders so that they would refer to the *ra'is* as the final arbiter.

In this environment, the PNA security sector witnessed a rapid proliferation. Very soon after its establishment, the PNA had ten different security organisations under its command: *Civil Police, Civil Defence, Preventive Security, National Security Forces, Naval Police, Aerial Police, Military Liaison, Military Intelligence, Presidential Security (Force 17),* and *General Intelligence.*

Except for the *Preventive Security*, these organisations were mostly based on PLO military units from the Diaspora; and they were official PNA organisations in the sense that they were explicitly or implicitly – such as *Aerial Police* and *Military Intelligence* – mentioned in the *Oslo Agreements I* (1994) and *II* (1995).

Later in the 1990s, Arafat then proceeded to establish new internal intelligence organisations that had not been provided for in the *Agreements*, such as *Special Security* and *Special Forces*, which brought the number of different bodies up to 12. In addition to that, many security organisations operated independent West Bank and Gaza branches, which meant that the number of autonomous security organisations was in reality even higher. The result was a massive inflation of personnel: by 1996, the PNA had more than 35,000 security officers on the payroll, even though *Oslo II* had limited the 'Palestinian Police Force' to 30,000.

Between 1994 and 2000, the performance of the PNA security organisations was mixed. Some branches worked in an effective and law-abiding mode – certainly by regional standards – and managed to maintain a modicum of law and order in the Areas A[7], despite the geographical and organisational constraints under which they had to operate. On a more general level, however, the work of the PNA security organisations was marred by confusion over remits and responsibilities, inefficiency and sometimes even open confrontation between different branches. Also, organisations with intelligence functions engaged in political repression and became distrusted. The absence of a legal framework and weak legislative and judicial oversight over the security sector meant that security personnel were rarely held accountable for violations of the law.

With the eruption of the second *Intifada*, Palestinian security sector governance became much more complicated. Between 2000 and 2002, Israel almost completely destroyed the security infrastructure of the PNA, including police stations, barracks, detention centres, vehicles and communications systems, thereby crippling all PNA capacity to uphold law and order in the areas under its control. Non-statutory security actors entered the scene at the same pace at which the PNA's administrative infrastructure disintegrated. Islamist armed groups such as the *Izz ad-Din al-Qassam Brigades* (Hamas) or the *Al-Quds Battalions* (Islamic Jihad in Palestine) started to combine their paramilitary activities with law-and-order functions; new actors emerged like the Fatah affiliated *Al-Aqsa Martyrs Brigades.*

Recognising the malfunctions in the PNA security sector, Palestinian reform politicians and academics relatively soon began to call for security reforms, namely in the late 1990s.[8] However, Arafat only started to act on that criticism after Israeli reoccupation of the West Bank in 2002 and under strong external pressure. In Spring 2002, he announced a '100-Day Plan' for administrative and security reforms which was based on recommendations by members of the Palestinian Legislative Council (PLC) and reform-minded Fatah officials. Key elements of the plan included the activation of the dormant Higher Council of National Security (HCNS) and the unification of three internal security organisations – *Civil Police*, *Preventive Security* and *Civil Defence* – under an empowered Ministry of the Interior. By imposing a shift from a strong presidential system to some form of parliamentary democracy, and the transfer of executive control to the newly-appointed Prime Minister, Israel, the US and some European allies hoped to loosen Arafat's grip on the security sector.

However, reality turned out quite differently: the internal organisations were indeed merged under a newly-appointed Minister of the Interior in late 2002, but the respective individuals never enjoyed any authority in their positions. All other security reforms remained cosmetic and were part of Arafat's effort to deflect political pressure and secure his position.

Following Arafat's death, the Palestinian leadership under President Mahmoud Abbas (Abu Mazen) was eager to break with the legacy of the former President. Abbas, in January 2005, made the reestablishment of the PNA's monopoly on force his declared priority task. His two-fold strategy aimed at accommodating the Islamist opposition and initiating institutional and organisational reforms in the security sector. Thereby Abbas also hoped to comply with the Palestinian security obligations under Phase I of the Road Map.[9]

President Abbas successfully coopted the opposition through dialogue and consensus. In March 2005, all Palestinian factions including Hamas and Islamic Jihad agreed in Cairo on a 'period of calm' (*tahdi'a*), a temporary ceasefire based on reciprocity. In exchange, Abbas promised Hamas and Islamic Jihad to become part of a politically and organisationally recalibratedPLO. This approach led to a significant decrease of violence in 2005. Hamas, the most important Islamist faction, largely respected the 'Cairo Agreement' and refrained from major operations against Israel.[10] The Palestinian factions furthermore showed remarkable restraint for the duration of Israel's 'disengagement' from Gaza and enabled the Israeli government to successfully carry out the withdrawal.

Compared to political progress, institutional reforms were much less impressive, partly because many activities were dictated by short-term needs in the context of the Israeli disengagement. The Palestinian leadership, supported by the US and Europe, concentrated its efforts on four areas.

1. Structural Reorganisation

The PNA, in April 2005, began to merge the numerous security forces into three main security organisations: The *Internal Security Forces,* the *National Security Forces,* and the *General Intelligence Organisation.* While the first two came under the authority of the Ministry of the Interior and National Security (MoINS), the *General Intelligence Organisation* remained under the command of the President (for a detailed description of the PNA security organisations and their structure see Appendix A). As many security organisations opposed their subordination to the Ministry of Interior and National Security, the new structure largely remained paperwork. Some influential individuals in the Ministry had a strong preference for more decentralised and loosely-structured security organisations, which ran counter to PNA policy of centralisation and institutionalisation. This weakened the Ministry of the Interior and undermined its control capacity.

In addition, President Abbas in April 2005 sent some 20 long-standing security commanders into retirement, in an effort to rejuvenate the security command. He also disbanded the *Special Forces* and the *Special Security* and made moves to re-activate the National Security Council (NSC). His plan was to turn it into the highest decision-making and coordinating body in security matters.

2. Establishing a Legal Framework for the Security Sector

The PNA made efforts towards establishing a normative-legal framework for the security sector. In autumn 2005, at the suggestion of various donors, the PNA Presidency started to work on a White Paper for the security sector. The draft included a threat assessment and plans for a force structure. In order to delineate responsibilities in the security sector, especially in relation to the security organisations and their oversight, the PNA developed first draft laws.

3. Civil Police Reform

With the help of European donors, the PNA initiated a *Civil Police* reform programme. In spring 2005, the EU deployed an advisory team to the region, which established in Ramallah the European Union Coordination Office for Palestinian Police Support (EUCOPPS). Its mission was to assist the PNA in improving its law-enforcement capacity.[11] EUCOPPS, in early 2005, delivered police vehicles and equipment and supported Palestinians with the reconstruction of communication systems and police stations.

4. Disarmament, Demobilisation and Reintegration (DDR)

The PNA embarked on a tentative DDR process, when Abbas ordered the *Al-Aqsa Martyrs Brigades* to become part of the official security forces. Subsequently, the PNA introduced various schemes of reintegration for Fatah militants in the West Bank and Gaza. The official policy was to enlist *Al-Aqsa* operatives on the PNA payroll, either as part of the security organisations or through monthly allowances. *Al-Aqsa* operatives also underwent training courses in preparation for their new functions.

The Security Sector under the Hamas Government

The ascension of Hamas to government sharply altered Palestinian relations with Israel and the donor community. Soon after the January elections in 2006, Israel and the Quartet made the transfer of customs and tax revenues and the continuation of financial aid to the PNA Government contingent upon Hamas' acceptance of three conditions: recognition of the State of Israel, renunciation of violence, and full acceptance of all agreements concluded between Israel and the PLO.

Hamas responded to these demands by offering a long-term *hudna* (ceasefire) with Israel and the partial recognition of Israeli-Palestinian agreements. Israel and the Quartet viewed these concessions as insufficient for freeing Hamas from the 'terror' label, with the result that the US and the EU stopped all financial and material support to the PNA Government and banned direct contact with its representatives.

Simultaneously, the US put pressure on foreign banks not to transfer money to the Government, and Israel withheld the transfer of tax revenues and customs.

The financial boycott of the PNA caused a severe deterioration in the economic situation in the Palestinian Territories. The cash-strapped Hamas Government was unable to pay the salaries of the 170,000 public employees, which provide income for some 1.2 million Palestinians; important sectors such as health and education, which are almost entirely run by the PNA, came under immense strain.

At the same time, tensions between Hamas and Fatah rose to a new high. Fatah, unable to accept its electoral defeat, set out to undermine the Hamas Government politically and organisationally, in the hope that it might return to power through new elections. Hamas, for its part, was determined to continue in government and undertook efforts to consolidate its rule. The stand-off between the Hamas and Fatah was accompanied by armed clashes and assassination campaigns.

As control over the security forces was at the core of this power struggle, the PNA President tried to remove the Fatah-dominated security organisations from the control of the Government. In an ironic twist, the Office of the President and Western governments tried to restore the structure of the security sector that had existed under Arafat. President Abbas separated the *National Security Forces* from the Ministry of the Interior and National Security and nominated a Chief-of-Staff[12] who reported directly to him. Furthermore, President Abbas nominated Brigadier-General Rashid Abu Shbak, until then Head of the *Preventive Security*, as Director-General for Internal Security in the Ministry of the Interior, making him the head of all three internal organisations (*Civil Police*, *Preventive Security*, and *Civil Defence*). In April 2006, Abbas also ordered the creation of a new 'Public Administration of the Crossing Points and Borders' under his control and appointed a loyalist as the head of the organisation. At the same time, the *Presidential Guard*, which had long been affiliated with the *Presidential Security/Force 17*, was expanded, provided with rapid-intervention capabilities and put under the direct control of the President.

The Hamas Government reacted to these steps in April 2006 with the creation of the so-called *Backup Force (Special Backup Force to the Police)*, a new security unit under the control of Minister of the Interior Said Siyam (Hamas). The *Backup Force*, renamed *Executive Force* soon afterwards, comprised initially some 3,000 operatives from the *Izz ad-Din al-Qassam Brigades*, the Popular Resistance Committees and its military wing, the *Nasser Salahaddin Brigades*, and a number of smaller factions.[13] On 6 January 2007, the Ministry of the Interior announced plans to increase the strength of the *Executive Force* from the 5,700 men it had by then reached to 12,000 personnel.[14] Its official mission is to support the existing security organisations in enforcing law and order in Gaza, but its establishment was foremost a reaction to Hamas' difficulties to assert control in the Fatah-dominated security sector. Hamas's move in turn encountered stiff opposition from the Office of the President and Fatah, which set up its own armed groups in parts of Gaza and the West Bank and recruited additional personnel into *Preventive Security* and other organisations.

For the Palestinian SSR process, Hamas' ascension to government had two consequences. Firstly, Palestinian-driven reform projects such as the legal framework for the security sector and the White Paper were put on hold. Secondly, most donors slowed down, stopped or reoriented their SSR-related assistance. The United States Security Coordinator (USSC), led in 2006 by Lieutenant General Keith Dayton, broke off all contacts with the PNA except for the Office of the President; USSC shifted its support towards border management issues in Gaza and the strengthening of the *Pres-*

idential Guard, with the aim of bolstering Abbas against the Hamas Government; the US also suspended planned programmes of community policing and strategic management support to the Ministry of the Interior. At the same time, US intelligence stepped up funding and technical assistance to Fatah and Fatah-controlled security organisations in Gaza. EUCOPPS also reduced its engagement with the *Civil Police*, but maintained a ground-presence in the Palestinian Territories.

The Continuing Need for Palestinian SSR

Since the rise of Hamas to power, Palestinian security sector governance has more than ever become hostage to the political dynamics of the region. However, the necessity of a thorough overhaul of the PNA security sector remains unchanged: Palestinians still lack basic human security and suffer from rampant lawlessness, crime and economic decline, as Gaza and parts of the West Bank are descending into a virtual state of anarchy. For the first time since the outbreak of the second *Intifada*, in 2005 the number of Palestinians killed in internal violence surpassed the number of those killed by Israel.

At the same time, the PNA security sector continues to suffer from major institutional deficiencies. Security organisations are accused of engaging in illegal rent-seeking, corruption and the violation of citizens' rights. Extreme politicisation of the security organisations and the domination of some branches by the Fatah movement compound these problems. Palestinians, across the political spectrum, demand comprehensive security reforms and the establishment of law and order. According to a poll conducted in spring 2006 by DCAF and the Geneva-based Graduate Institute for Development Studies (IUED), Palestinians overwhelmingly want less corrupt, more efficient, rights-respecting security organisations. They attach great value to increased civil-democratic management and oversight and want the Palestinian parliament to play a role in it.[15]

A de-politicised, accountable and effective PNA security sector also remains crucial for the political viability of the PNA. In combination with the dissolution of institutions that was set off by the international boycott of the Hamas Government, this is likely to pose grave danger to the institutional set-up of the PNA. Unless Palestinian factions join forces, compromise on the sharing of power and restore the functioning of their institutions, the PNA and the state formation process are exposed to grave danger.

Outline of the Book

The present volume is divided into six chapters that deal with various aspects of Palestinian security sector governance.

The *first chapter* examines the legal framework of the PNA security sector. Asem Khalil analyses in detail the recent legislative efforts in the security domain, in par-

18

ticular the laws regulating the functions of the different security organisations, and puts them in the context of the existing constitutional framework. While appreciating the reform process and acknowledging the importance of a sound legal basis for the security sector, Khalil cautions against a narrow legal-technical approach to SSR. He argues that Palestinian security sector governance presents multi-faceted challenges to policy-makers, and the best legal framework is of little use if not implemented in practice.

The *second chapter* examines how the security sector reform process relates to the security organisations and the PNA Executive. The author critically analyses the performance of the security organisations before the SSR process and evaluates its impact. He also reviews the role of external actors and their involvement in the reform process. Drawing on his experience as a security practitioner, the author proposes a detailed reform strategy for overhauling the executive pillar of the PNA security sector. Without sufficient planning capabilities and sustained international assistance, he argues, it will be impossible to strengthen executive control over the security organisations.

In the *third chapter*, Majed Arouri and Mamoun Attili examine civil-democratic oversight mechanisms in the security sector. The authors analyse the legislative, legal and civil society dimensions of oversight. They identify three major deficiencies: the lack of appropriate legal tools, a decade of single-party domination of the PLC, and the centralisation of security sector governance under Arafat. After 2004, they attest to the PLC's increasing willingness and efforts to monitor the activities of the security organisations. (See also Appendix B, which contains a translation of the first comprehensive PLC report on security sector governance after Arafat). Effective judicial review, the authors suggest, is still missing in the Palestinian Territories because the PNA Judiciary remains politicised and lacks the necessary capacities to exercise oversight. Arouri and Attili further argue that Palestinian civil society, regardless of how important its monitoring role has been, cannot replace functioning legislative and judicial mechanisms of oversight.

The *fourth chapter* looks at the often neglected relationship between SSR and judicial reform. Maen Id'ais describes the PNA judiciary reforms and critically examines their impact. He analyses both the legal framework and the cooperation between the Judiciary and the security organisations. Id'ais argues that PNA judicial reforms have been mainly rhetorical, despite the PNA having declared them a priority. He draws attention to the dysfunctional relations between the *Civil Police* and the Public Prosecution and the extra-legal activities of the PNA intelligence organisations. Both, he says, undermine the rule of law.

In the *fifth chapter*, Mohammad Najib and Roland Friedrich examine the role of non-statutory actors in Palestinian security sector governance, arguably one of the greatest challenges of SSR. Najib and Friedrich describe the origins, ideology, strategy and capabilities of the politically most relevant non-state armed groups, namely the military wings of Hamas, Palestinian Islamic Jihad and the Popular Resistance Committees, as well as the *Al-Aqsa Martyrs Brigades*. The authors argue that non-statutory armed groups have always been a feature of PNA security sector governance, but have been able to raise their profile during and after the second *Intifada*. Najib and Friedrich look at how Palestinians might deal with non-statutory armed groups and conclude that integration into the PNA security organisations is the only feasible strategy.

The *sixth chapter* presents a Hamas view on reforms needed in the PNA. Ghazi Hamad contributed this chapter only shortly after Hamas had won the elections and found itself confronted with the challenge of delivering on its electoral promise of change and reform. At that time Hamas believed that it would be given a chance to demonstrate its commitment on reform. Hamad describes how Hamas planned to use its electoral victory to bring transparency and accountable management to the security sector. His inside description pictures Hamas as a political actor that recognises the need for better governance in the PNA and sees the strengthening of transparency and accountability as a key task. He analyses the challenges that the management of domestic priorities and external constraints poses to Hamas in government and outlines Hamas' phased reform strategy which is organised around three pillars: securing the truce with Israel; managing relations with Fatah; and improving governance in priority areas such as adjudication, parliamentary monitoring and executive planning.

The *final chapter* in this volume attempts to synthesise the assessments and suggestions made by the authors into a set of recommendations on how to advance Palestinian SSR. It highlights various entry-points to SSR, which Palestinians and the donor community could use for strengthening security sector governance in the Palestinian Territories.

Notes

1   Involving beneficiaries in all stages of the security sector reform process is also one of the key conclusions of the Development Assistance Committee (DAC) of the OECD, which in its handbook suggests measures for enhancing local ownership. For more details see *OECD DAC Handbook on Security System Reform: Supporting Security and Justice* (Paris: OECD DAC, 2007).

2   United Nations Development Programme (UNDP), *Human Development Report 2002: Deepening democracy in a fragmented world* (Oxford University Press: Oxford, 2002), p. 87.

3   For a broad definition of the security sector see also OECD DAC guidelines on SSR. *DAC Guidelines and Reference Series: Security System Reform and Governance* (Paris: OECD DAC, 2005), p. 20-21.

4   The *Executive Force* was established by the Hamas-led Palestinian Ministry of the Interior. Although President Mahmoud Abbas in Summer 2006 agreed to put 5,700 members of the *Executive Force* on the PNA payroll, the legitimacy of the organisation has remained contested by Fatah and the Office of the President.

5   See also Hänggi, H. (2003), 'Making Sense of Security Sector Governance', in: Bryden, A. and Hänggi, H., *Challenges of Security Sector Governance* (Münster: Lit Verlag, 2003), p. 10.

6   OECD DAC defines 'security sector reform' as "the transformation of this sector so that it is managed and operates in a manner that is more consistent with democratic norms, the rule of law including well-functioning and just judicial and prison systems, and sound principles of governance". See also Hänggi, H. (2003), p. 17.

7   In the *Oslo* terminology, Area A referred to the Gaza Strip (minus the Israeli settlements) and the urban areas in the West Bank where the PNA had explicit jurisdiction under *Oslo* II.

8   For example, in 1999 the Independent Task Force on Strengthening Palestinian Public Institutions published a report that addressed various shortcomings in the PNA's performance in the security domain. Independent Task Force Report, *Strengthening Palestinian Public Institutions*, Yezid Sayigh/Khalil Shikaki, Principal Authors, New York 1999, pp. 73-78.

9   The 'Road Map' is a gradualist peace plan consisting of three phases, issued by the Quartet of Middle East mediators in April 2003 (the Quartet comprises the US, the European Union (EU), the Russian Federation, and the United Nations (UN)). Under Phase I, the 'Road Map' calls for a 'rebuilt and refocused Palestinian Authority security apparatus' and requires the PNA to undertake 'visible efforts on the ground to arrest, disrupt, and restrain individuals and groups conducting and planning violent attacks on Israelis anywhere'. The PNA is also obliged to dismantle the capability and infrastructure of paramilitary groups through weapons confiscation and arrests. See *A Performance-Based Roadmap to a Permanent Two-State Solution to the Israeli-Palestinian Conflict*, 30 April 2003.

10   Islamic Jihad had a more ambiguous record of various suicide bombings and continuing low-scale attacks on Israel. However, the Jihad's political leadership constantly underlined its commitment to peace and said that it was merely reacting to Israeli military operations.

11   EUCOPPS is set to last for three years and to be composed of 33 senior European police officers. The mission of EUCOPPS is two-fold: to assist the PNA in the short term with strengthening the public order and anti-crime capabilities of the *Civil Police*; and to support the long-term transformation of the *Civil Police* in order to bring it into line with civil-democratic policing standards. See EUCOPPS/PNA Ministry of Interior, *Palestinian Civil Police Development Programme, Transformational and Operational Plans 2005-2008*.

12   The positions of Chief of Staff and Director-General of Internal Security had been created through the *Law of Service in the Palestinian Security Forces No. 8 of 2005* and had been vacant until then.

13   The Minister of the Interior had originally slated Jamal Abu Samhadana, Head of the Popular Resistance Committees, to command the force, until Samhadana was killed in an Israeli air strike in early June 2006.

14   Najib, M., 'Hamas-led PA expands Executive Force', in: Jane's Defence Weekly, 15.01.2007.

15   Roland Friedrich, Arnold Luethold, Luigi de Martino, *Government Change and Security Sector Governance: Palestinian Public Perceptions, Summary Report*, 3 August 2007, (Geneva: DCAF-IUED). Available at: http://ww.dcaf.ch/mena/Palestine_Sec_Perceptions.pdf.

The Legal Framework for Palestinian Security Sector Governance

Asem Khalil

The *Amended Basic Law of 2003* stipulates: *'The security forces and the police shall be regulated by law.'*[1] This clause was already present in the very early drafts of the Palestinian 'quasi-constitution'. Yet, after more than ten years of Palestinian self-rule, there is little legislation regulating the work of the security organisations of the Palestinian National Authority (PNA). In fact, they still operate in a partial legal vacuum.

As the Israeli-Palestinian agreements provided the basis for the establishing of the security organisations, the PNA felt little need to endow them with a sound legal basis. It was only after the outbreak of the second *Intifada* in 2000 that the absence of a legal framework for the PNA security sector became a problem. The deteriorating security situation and the rise of armed groups called for efficient security organisations. But in order to build stronger security organisations, their mandates and accountability mechanisms needed to be defined by law. Rather reluctantly, the late PNA President Yasser Arafat in August 2004 called upon the Palestinian Legislative Council (PLC) *'to elaborate the necessary laws to ensure an efficient and controlled working of the security forces.'*[2]

SSR in the Palestinian Context

The *Oslo* period, during which a negotiated solution of the Israeli-Palestinian conflict was to be reached, ended in 2000 without any permanent agreement. However, during the following years the Palestinians continued to prepare for statehood, with the PNA acting as if it had full sovereignty over the West Bank and Gaza. This gave the PNA a quasi-state character, despite its very limited and fragmented territorial jurisdiction.

At the same time, Palestinians started to call for more democracy and began to look towards elections as the way for putting their house in order. Accelerated by the inauguration of a new President, municipal elections were held in 2004 and 2005 and legislative elections in January 2006.

Palestinian public and leadership attitudes towards the PNA security organisations also changed. Rather than simply an instrument for implementing the security obligations of the *Oslo Agreements*, the PNA security organisations came to be seen as the embryonic security and defence apparatus of a future Palestinian state.

These state-building efforts contrasted sharply with political realities on the ground, where Israeli policies created facts, which made the establishment of a viable Palestinian state increasingly less likely.

The 'Constitutional' Framework and its Ambiguities

The *Oslo II Agreement (1995)* provided for the adoption of a *Basic Law* by the PLC. However, the scope of the *Basic Law* was to be limited to issues dealt with in *Oslo II*.[3] In other words, the *Basic Law* is not the constitution of a sovereign state but a transitional document which is to be replaced by a Palestinian constitution once statehood is attained.[4] This is despite the fact that the PNA and the PLC managed to increase their popular legitimacy through elections.

In this context, the creation of a legal framework for the PNA security sector, as called for in the *Amended Basic Law (2003)*, was difficult for three reasons. Firstly, almost all issues relating to security governance were already regulated in the *Oslo Agreements*. Secondly, *Oslo II* restricted new legislation. It explicitly stated that any legislation exceeding the jurisdiction of the PLC '*shall have no effect and shall be void ab initio.*'[5] This left little room for the PLC. It also banned the PNA President from promulgating any Palestinian legislation which contradicted the Agreements.[6] Thirdly, Arafat, from a very early stage on, monopolised all security decisions. He could invoke the *Oslo Agreements* which invested the PNA President with large powers, such as vast administrative authority and a veto to block PLC legislation.[7] The PLC was thus unable to issue legislation in any field that the President considered his prerogative.

The Beginning of the Palestinian SSR Process

Pressured by Palestinian reformers and the international community during the *Intifada,* the late Arafat reluctantly acquiesced in institutional and security reforms. In 2002, he created the post of Minister of the Interior and gave the PNA Cabinet responsibility for ensuring 'public order and internal security'[8]; this was a significant step towards parliamentary oversight because the *Basic Law* enabled the PLC to censure ministers through motions of confidence.[9] Arafat also ordered three internal security organisations – *Civil Police, Preventive Security* and *Civil Defence* – to be placed under the control of the Ministry of the Interior.

The following year, Arafat approved the creation of the post of the PNA Prime Minister which was envisaged to take over responsibility for domestic governance. In 2004, he issued a decree calling for the unification of all PNA security organisations into three branches: 1. *National Security Forces (NSF)*, 2. *Internal Security Forces (ISF)*, including *Civil Police, Preventive Security* and *Civil Defence*, and 3. *General Intelligence (GI)*.

However, the practical impact of these reforms was rather limited. Until his last day Arafat continued to exercise direct control over the Palestinian security sector. Although a legal justification for this could be found in the *Basic Law* – *Article 39* states that the PNA President is the Commander-in-Chief of all Palestinian security organisations –, Arafat's dominating role in security and security sector governance was primarily a function of power and customary practice; since he had become the lynchpin of Palestinian politics in the 1970s, Arafat considered the PLO and later the PNA security sector crucial pillars of his rule, and he was very reluctant to yield any control over them. This virtually precluded any efforts at institutionalisation and reform.[10]

The Legal Framework for Security Sector Governance

The legal framework of the PNA security sector currently includes security laws enacted prior to the establishment of the PNA and security laws enacted by the PNA. The first group of laws stems mainly from British, Egyptian and Jordanian legislation.[11] Some of these laws still remain in force, whereas others have been totally or partially replaced by PLC legislation or PNA presidential decrees.[12] The second group includes laws which directly regulate the structure and authority of the various security organisations and their relations to the Executive, Legislature and Judiciary. It further includes laws which regulate the security organisations indirectly, because they also apply to other sectors of the PNA. These include the *Law of the Organisation of the General Budget and Public Finance No. 7 of 1998*, the *Public Meetings Law No. 12 of 1998*, the *Law of the Judicial Authority No. 1 of 2002*, the *Penal Procedure Law No. 3 of 2001*, the *Law of the Formation of Regular Courts No. 5 of 2001*, and the *Law of Illegal Gains No. 1 of 2005*.

Legal Development Efforts since 2004

Following Arafat's replacement, the PLC made increased efforts to amend and complete the legal framework for the security sector. In 2004 and 2005, the PNA enacted four laws that regulated human-resources management in the security sector for the first time. In an effort to institutionalise its security branches, the PNA also began to draft laws for the individual organisations, one of which was approved in 2005 (see Table 1).

Table 1:   The Current Legal Framework for the PNA Security Sector

Law	Subject	Adopted in PLC	Referred to President	Ratified on	Ratified by President	Date of Publication in Official Gazette
No. 2 (1998)	Firearms and Ammunition	02.04.1998 (2nd reading)	20.04.1998	20.05.1998	ARAFAT	08. 06.1998 (No.23)
No. 3 (1998)	Civil Defence	31.09.1998 (2nd reading)	20.04.1998	28.05.1998		01.07.1998 (No. 24)
No. 6 (1998)	Correction and Rehabilitation Centres ('Prisons')	28.04.1998 (2nd reading)	02.05.1998	28.05.1998		01.07.1998 (No. 24)
No. 12 (1998)	Public Meetings	25.11.1998 (2nd reading)	19.12.1998	28.12.1998		13.03.1998 (No. 28)
No. 16 (2004)	Insurance and Pensions of the Palestinian Security Forces	22.12.2004 (3rd reading)	07.10.2004	28.12.2004	FATTOUH	28.02.2005 (No. 53)
No. 3 (2005)	Amending Parts of Law No. 6 (1998)	08.12.2004 (2nd reading)	11.01.2005	11.01.2005		23.04.2005 (No. 54)
No. 7 (2005)	Public Retirement	07.04.2005	11.04.2005	26.04.2005	ABBAS	27.06.2005 (No. 55)
No. 8 (2005)	Service in the Palestinian Security Forces	11.05.2005	14.05.2005	04.06.2005		28.06.2005 (No. 56)
No. 16 (2005)	Amending Parts of Law No. 16 (2004)	21.09.2005		23.10.2005		09.11.2005 (No. 60)
No. 17 (2005)	General Intelligence	21.09.2005		26.10.2005		09.11.2005 (No. 60)

Despite these efforts, by the end of 2005, only two security organisations – the *General Intelligence* and the *Civil Defence* – had their own laws. Draft laws for other security organisations were circulating in various stages of advancement; the *National Security Forces Draft Law* and the *Civil Police Draft Law* had been submitted to the PLC together with the *General Intelligence Draft Law* in February 2005, and the *Preventive Security Draft Law* was submitted to the PLC for general discussion in January 2006. As of May 2007, these draft laws were still awaiting approval.

The Council of Ministers (Cabinet) approved and transferred to the PLC the draft of a *Basic Security Law* in October 2005. This so-called 'umbrella law' is set to regulate the general structure of the security sector, including the responsibilities of the various agencies and civilian control. The draft presents several weaknesses. In its current state, some provisions of the draft conflict with existing security legislation, especially the *Law of Service in the Palestinian Security Forces No. 8 of 2005*. The draft of the *Basic Security Law* also contains controversial provisions in relation to the tasks and remits of the security organisations and the delineation of responsibilities between the President and the Minister of the Interior. According to the draft text, future amendments of the law would require a two-thirds majority. This would limit how major a role the PLC could play in the security domain. Moreover, although making reference to the National Security Council (NSC), the *Basic Security Draft Law* neither regulates its structure and mission, nor refers to the existing *National Security Council Draft Law* or the *Presidential Decree Concerning Reforming the National Security Council of 2005*. For these reasons and because the *Basic Security Draft Law* is likely to undergo significant changes in the PLC, it is not included in the comparative analysis below.

Functions of the PNA Security Organisations

A key rationale for the legislation efforts that began in 2004 was to define the responsibilities of the security organisations in the light of the rather generic provisions in the *Basic Law*, which addresses security sector governance only cursorily in *Article 84*:

'The security forces and the police are regular armed forces, created as a service to the people, for the protection of the homeland and society, and for the maintenance of security and public order. They shall perform their duties, within the limits provided by law, with full respect to rights and freedoms.'

The current legal framework defines the responsibilities of the security organisations as follows:

- The *Civil Police* has the task of protecting public order and preventing crime. In the absence of PNA police legislation, Jordanian and Egyptian laws serve as the legal basis: in the West Bank, this is the *Jordanian Temporary Law No. 38 of 1965 Regarding Public Security*, in Gaza it is the *Egyptian Law No. 6 of 1963*. Both laws apply separately to Gaza and the West Bank.
- The responsibilities of the *General Intelligence*, as defined in *Article 9 General Intelligence Law No. 17 of 2005*, include: preventing 'any acts that may place the

security and safety of Palestine in danger'; 'combating external threats to Palestinian national security such as espionage and sabotage'; and 'cooperation with similar agencies of friendly states.'

- The mission of the *Preventive Security*, according to its draft law, includes: upholding internal security and combating internal threats against the PNA, including those aimed at international agreements; fighting regular crime; fighting economic crime and combating corruption; and counter-espionage.
- The *Civil Defence* is responsible for civil protection and emergency services. According to *Article 3* of the *Civil Defence Law No. 3 of 1998* this includes the safety of communications and the protection of public and private infrastructure from 'air raids, natural catastrophes, and fire.'

The existing legislation is incomplete and reflects more the status quo than a comprehensive vision of security. The mission of the *National Security Forces* is not yet defined by law and the *National Security Forces Draft Law* still awaits parliamentary approval. The stated responsibilities of the *Preventive Security* largely overlap with the missions of the *General Intelligence* and the *Civil Police*. Some agencies, as for instance the *General Intelligence*, had their prerogatives written into law. On the positive side, however, the current legal framework reflects sincere efforts to depoliticise the security organisations. For example, the *Law of Service in the Palestinian Security Forces No. 8 of 2005* bans security officers from political activities[13]; similar provisions are included in *Article 25 (5)* of the *General Intelligence Law No. 17 of 2005*. This is an important step, given that some security agencies resemble in fact political[14] militias.

Structure of the PNA Security Organisations

Up to now, Palestinian legislation has not provided a comprehensive framework for security sector governance. Only the *Law of Service in the Palestinian Security Forces No. 8 of 2005* regulates the security sector. Read in conjunction with the remaining legislation, the *Law of Service in the Palestinian Security Forces* organises the security sector as follows (see Table 2):

- The PNA security organisations consist of three branches: *Internal Security Forces (ISF), National Security Forces (NSF)*, and *General Intelligence (GI) (Article 3)*. The article also states that *'any other existing or future force or forces will be integrated into one of these three forces.'* However, the article defines neither the mission of these forces, nor their mutual relations.
- The legal distinction between 'military forces' (NSF) and 'security forces' (ISF) indicates a willingness to differentiate between internal and external security functions, assigning them to the Ministries of the Interior and National Security respectively. This provision is in contradiction with *Article 1* of the *National Security Forces Draft Law*, which stipulates that the *National Security Forces* report directly to the President.

- The *General Intelligence* remains independent. The head of the organisation reports directly to the President. He enjoys broad discretionary powers. *Article 3* of the *General Intelligence Law No. 17 of 2005* confers on the head of the *General Intelligence* a ministerial rank.
- The President has the prerogative to appoint the heads of the security organisations. His appointments are not subject to an approval procedure. According to *Article 69 (7)* of the *Amended Basic Law (2003)*, the Cabinet only has the right to propose a candidate for the position of the Director-General of Internal Security (DGIS).[15]
- The law limits the term of office for top security commanders to three years, extendable for one year only. The commanders keep direct control over the internal organisation of their agencies.

However, the *Law of Service in the Palestinian Security Forces* is essentially a technical text. Functional differentiations between all components of the security sector would need to be laid down in a *Basic Security Law*. It is therefore no wonder that the current legal framework has many inconsistencies. For example, the relations between the Director-General of Internal Security (DGIS) and the heads of the three internal security organisations are not clear from the law. The *Law of Service in the Palestinian Security Forces* puts the DGIS in direct command of all three internal agencies; however, the *Civil*

Defence Law No. 6 of 1998 puts the *Civil Defence* directly under the Minister of the Interior *(Article 3),* and the *Civil Police* and *Preventive Security Draft Laws* do not mention the DGIS at all.

Table 2: *Structure of the Security Sector according to the Law of Service in the Palestinian Security Forces*

	National Security Forces	Internal Security Forces	General Intelligence
Articles	7 & 8	10 & 11	13 & 14
Definition	'A regular military organisation'	'A regular security organisation'	'A regular independent security organisation reporting to the President'
Political control *(ri'asa)*	Minister of National Security	Minister of Interior	Head of General Intelligence (with ministerial rank, but not member of the Cabinet)
Command *(qiyada)*	Commander-in-Chief	Director-General of Internal Security (position vacant until April 2006)	Head of General Intelligence
Appointment of commander	By presidential decree	By presidential decree on nomination *(tanseeb)* of the Council of Ministers	By presidential decree
Term of duty for commander	Three years; one-year extension possible	Three years; one-year extension possible	Three years; one-year extension possible
Authority of commander	'(...) shall issue forth the decisions necessary for the administration of its work and regulation of all of its affairs, in accordance with the provisions of the Law and regulations issued therewith.'	'(...) shall issue forth the decisions necessary for the administration of its work and regulation of all of its affairs.'	'(...) shall also issue forth the decisions necessary for the administration of its work and regulation of all of its affairs.'

The National Security Council (NSC)

In an effort to deflect domestic criticism of his autocratic rule over the security sector, Arafat established in 2003 the National Security Council. He did this by reactivating and reorganising the dormant 'Higher Council of National Security'[16] established in 1994. Members of the NSC included Arafat as its Chairman, the Prime Minister, Ministers of the Cabinet and the top security commanders. In legal terms, the status of the NSC was problematic; established by presidential decree, it sought to replace the 'constitutional' responsibility of the Cabinet for upholding 'public order and internal security' *(Article 69 (7), Amended Basic Law 2003)*; but was itself an un-constitutional body without any legal basis. In practice, legal considerations were irrelevant, as Arafat continued to control the security branches directly.

In November 2004, Interim President Rawhi Fattouh transferred the chairmanship of the NSC to the Prime Minister. However, President Mahmoud Abbas issued in September 2005 a presidential decree by which he transferred the chairmanship back.[17] In his decree, he defined the functions of the NSC as follows:

- Formulation of security policies and plans;
- Threat identification and assessment;
- Coordination between political authorities and security commanders;
- Supervision of security cooperation with external actors;
- Security budget approval.[18]

Ironically, the PNA prepared at the same time a *NSC Draft Law* which adopted large parts of the mission statement from Abbas' decree, but placed the NSC again under the chairmanship of the Prime Minister.

For political reasons, the NSC has remained inactive since 2005. The NSC's structural relations with the security organisations have still not been defined. Yet, the NSC could prove important for Palestinian security decision-making in the future. Well-placed to coordinate the various actors, the NSC could become a sponsor and driver for SSR. Several preparatory steps are required to activate the NSC:

- The *Basic Law* needs to be amended to give the NSC a sound constitutional basis and to define its relationship with the Cabinet.
- For reasons of accountability, it is preferable that the Prime Minister head the NSC. In virtue of *Articles 74-79* of the *Amended Basic Law (2003)*, he would then become accountable to the PLC.[19]
- Following the amendment of the *Basic Law*, a specific NSC Law should be adopted for regulating the relations between the NSC and the security organisations. Alternatively, this could be done also through an amendment of the *Basic Security Draft Law*.

Addressing the Implementation Gap

If Palestinian SSR is to succeed, a comprehensive approach to security sector reform must be taken. Creating a legal framework for security sector governance is a crucial step but by itself not sufficient. A mere focus on the legal-technical aspects of SSR increases the risk of legislation becoming the target of reform rather than its tool.[20]

A comprehensive approach to SSR first of all means that the PNA Executive must live up to its legal responsibilities and not to the interests of certain political actors or influential individuals. The government must ensure the practical application of security legislation through all administrative channels and in particular through the security organisations. The Minister of the Interior should assume the main responsibility for security and coordinate the implementation of reforms with all other stakeholders. The PNA President's role should be limited to facilitating and ensuring the harmonious cooperation between all Palestinian institutions and factions in SSR. Such a division of labour would also bring the Palestinian political system closer to the model of parliamentary democracy, which is the best guarantee for strong civil-democratic oversight.

A positive and supportive attitude of the PNA security commanders is crucial for the success of SSR; they have the power to spoil or facilitate reform. It is therefore vital that security commanders be committed to reform and help translate political decisions into practice. The security organisations need to overcome factional loyalties and develop a real national and professional ethos. Internal accountability mechanisms in the PNA security organisations must be strengthened.

At the same time, the legitimate interest of security personnel needs to be taken into account. This means that the political authorities cannot simply impose reform measures; rather, security officers need to be actively involved in SSR through information and consultation. In this, special attention must be given to remuneration issues, training needs and the physical safety of security personnel and their families. However, it should be kept in mind that real SSR also carries costs; many of those who benefit from the current system will lose their privileges.

The PLC and the Judiciary need to be overhauled, before a functioning oversight system can be put in place. The PLC should quickly amend and adopt the remaining security laws in order to create a strong legal framework. The Council should also draft and adopt legislation for the PNA Military Courts, which have so far escaped reform.[21] Furthermore, the PNA President should officially abolish the State Security Courts which have long been operating beyond any procedural safeguards.[22] In addition to that, the PLC should make effective use of the oversight instruments at its disposal. Regular updates of the Council by the government and increased hearings and debates on security sector activities are long overdue. The enforcement of the rule of law through an efficient justice system remains another priority. Courts must protect the rights of citizens and rulings must be implemented.

Finally, responsibility for addressing the implementation gap also falls on society itself. Legal reform often requires a change of cultural patterns. Much remains to be done for Palestinians in this area, as is evident from the ambiguous attitude to the issue of corruption; the Palestinian public considers fighting corruption a top priority, but practices of illegal rent-seeking are hardly challenged socially.

Conclusion

The PNA has undertaken some important steps over the past two years towards the creation of a legal framework for the security sector, which deserve to be commended. Despite many shortcomings, the current legal framework provides guidance to security practitioners. However, for strengthening oversight it is important to strengthen the institutions and this requires improvements in the legal framework.

Notes

1. *Amended Basic Law (2003), Article 84 (2).*
2. Al-Tannini, M., 'Changes in the Palestinian Security Forces {Arabic}', *Majallat Markez al-Takhteet al-Filastini,* 2005, p. 18. Available at: http://www.oppc.pna.net/mag/mag18/p3-18.htm (Accessed 14 January 2005).
3. *The Israeli-Palestinian Interim Agreement on the West Bank and the Gaza Strip (1995), Article 3 (7).* The *Agreement* is referred to as *Oslo II* in the following.
4. The drafting of the *Basic Law* started with the declaration of Palestinian statehood by the PLO in Algiers in 1988 and continued in the context of *Oslo II.* Between 2001 and 2003, the PNA then prepared and published three drafts of a Palestinian constitution.
5. *Oslo II, Article 18(4).*
6. Ibid.
7. The 'presidential veto' could take two forms: the President refusing to sign a law, or the President signing a law but refusing to 'issue' it officially in the Palestinian Gazette.
8. *Amended Basic Law (2003), Article 69 (7).*
9. See *Amended Basic Law (2003), Articles 77-79.*
10. See PICCR, *The Status of the Palestinian Citizens' Rights during 2004. The Tenth Annual Report,* Ramallah 2005, p. 101.
11. Israeli military orders, issued between 1967 and 1994, were abrogated by presidential decree after the establishment of the PNA.
12. PNA laws replaced the following pieces of legislation over the last few years: *Law of Arms No. 20 of 1922* including its Gaza amendments; *Law of Arms and Munitions No. 34 of 1952* including its West Bank amendments; *Salary and Insurance Order Law No. 8 of 1964*; *PLO Executive Committee Chairman Order No. 6 of 1974*, including the *Pension Law for Palestine Liberation Army (PLA) Officers*; *PLO Executive Committee Chairman Order No. 7 of 1974 Regarding the Pension Law for PLA Officers and Soldiers.*
13. *Article 90*: 'During military service, the officer shall be prohibited from:
    1. Expressing political opinions and working in politics or affiliated with parties, entities, associations or organisations with political objectives.
    2. Participating in any demonstration or disturbances.
    3. Taking part in the organising of partisan meetings or electoral campaigns.'
14. The *Preventive Security*, for instance, has been described as the 'practical expression of Fatah.' Kelly, T., *Law, Coercion and Dispute Resolution: The Fragmentation of the Palestinian Legal System from the Oslo Peace Process to the Intifada,* Development Studies Institute, London School of Economics, 2003, p. 8. Available at: http://www.crisisstates.com/download/seminars/kelly.pdf (Accessed 14 January 2005).
15. However, here there are inconsistencies between the *Law of Service in the Palestinian Security Forces* and the *Civil Police* and *Preventive Security Draft Laws.* According to the *Preventive Security Draft Law*, the President nominates the Director-General of Preventive Security (DGPS) upon the recommendation of the Minister of the Interior, while the Minister himself appoints the DGPS's deputy (*Articles 13-14*). The *Civil Police Draft Law* states that the Cabinet appoints the Chief of Police upon the recommendation of the Minister of the Interior (*Article 5*). However, the *Law of Service in the Palestinian Security Forces* gives the right of appointment for both positions to the Minister of the Interior upon the recommendation of the Director-General of Internal Security (*Article 12*).
16. The Higher Council for National Security, established in 1994, was supposed to coordinate the work of the nascent PNA security branches and included the heads and deputy heads of all security organisations.
17. *Presidential Decree Concerning Reforming the National Security Council (2005).* According to the decree, the exact tasks of the NSC are as follows:

- 'To formulate security policies and plans based on the decisions of the President and supervise their implementation.
- To identify the security responsibilities of the PNA on the basis of the political, economic and social threat environment.
- To coordinate the work on the political and the security level and to ensure cohesion between both levels.
To approve the restructuring of forces and the transferral and promotion of personnel.
To approve the security budgets and supervise security expenditure.
To directly supervise security coordination with local, regional and international authorities.'
See also: Brown, N. J., 2005, *Evaluating Palestinian Reform*, Carnegie Paper No. 59 (June 2005), p. 16. Available at: http://www.carnegieendowment.org/files/CP59.brown.FINAL.pdf (Accessed 14 January 2005).

18 The NSC comprises the President, the Prime Minister, the Ministers of the Interior, Foreign Affairs, Civil Affairs and Finance, the National Security Adviser, and the Head of the PLO Negotiations Department. The commanders of the security organisations can be summoned to attend sessions.

19 See also Shikaki, K., *National Security Council: an ineffective and unconstitutional Institution that should be dissolved* {Arabic}, PCPSR (Palestinian Center for Public Survey and Reseach, Paper No. 13 (June 2004). Available at: http://www.pcpsr.org/arabic/strategic/papers/2004/no13.pdf (Accessed 14 January 2005).

20 Bahaa-Eddin, Z., 'Legal and Institutional Constraints Affecting Economic Reform', Newsletter of the Economic Research Forum for the Arab Countries, Iran and Turkey, Vol. 11 No. 2 (2005), pp. 16-19, p. 16. Available at: http://www.erf.org.eg/nletter/Newsletter_Sum04/NewForum-NewsSum04-P16.pdf (Accessed 14 January 2005).

21 Military Courts are provided for in *Article 101 (2) Amended Basic Law (2003)* which gives the PLC the right to establish military judiciary institutions. The *Law of Service in the Palestinian Security Forces No. 8 of 2005* mentions Military Courts in *Article 95*. Military Courts have jurisdiction over crimes perpetrated by PNA security personnel and disciplinary matters; they operate on the basis of the *PLO Revolutionary Penal Code of 1979* and the *PLO Revolutionary Criminal Procedures Law of 1979*.

22 The State Security Courts were formed in 1995 by Arafat and deal with cases relating to regime security. The High State Security Court is based on *Order No. 55 of 1964 of the Egyptian Governor-General of the Gaza Strip* which itself refers to British Emergency Laws from the mandate period. In the West Bank, the State Security Courts apply the *Jordanian Penal Code of 1960* and the *Jordanian Criminal Procedures Act of 1961*. In Gaza, the courts apply the *Mandate Penal Code of 1936* and the *PLO Revolutionary Penal Code of 1979*. The status of the State Security Courts is unclear. In 2003, the Ministry of Justice abrogated them by decree and transferred all pending cases to regular courts. However, there has been no presidential cancellation of the 1995 decree. Also, the PNA does not fully implement the decision of the Ministry of Justice: Regular courts only reviewed a part of the sentences made by the High State Security Court in Gaza, and in June 2005 President Abbas approved the execution of four individuals one of whom was convicted by the State Security Court in Gaza in 2000. *PICCR, Status of Citizens' Rights*, p. 84.

Reconstructing the PNA Security Organisations

Ahmad Hussein

Much has been said and written lately about the state and the performance of the Palestinian security sector, especially with respect to its structures, mechanisms and capabilities. The bulk of comments and assessments have been rather negative. Indeed, there are a variety of factors which account for the mixed performance of the PNA (Palestinian National Authority) security organisations and the loss of public confidence in their capacities, especially after the outbreak of violence between Palestinians and Israelis in September 2000.

Following the return of the PLO to the homeland in 1994, the PNA established various security organisations. The aim was to translate the achievements and experiences of the Palestinian resistance movements inside and outside Palestine into a strategy that would enable the PNA to assert control over the territory that it was designated to govern under the *Oslo Agreements*. The PNA security leadership was expected to devise a Palestinian national security policy that would lay out a plan for tackling the intricate Palestinian security situation and establishing an independent Palestinian state on the basis of a just peace agreement with Israel.

However, it soon became obvious that the reality in Palestine was going to be completely different. Policies that had had a certain logic during the PLO's exile were uncritically transferred to the new situation. For instance, the PNA created parallel organisations with identical functions so as to encourage competition and to ensure political control. This weakened the capacities of the PNA security sector from the beginning. The outbreak of the second *Intifada* in 2000 further degraded the capacities of the security agencies while the armed Palestinian opposition took the opportunity to improve its capabilities. Clearly, Israel played a very influential and negative role in this regard by its wholesale destruction of the PNA security infrastructure.

The end of the second *Intifada* in 2005 has provided the Palestinians with an opportunity to reconstruct and rehabilitate their security sector with international help, despite continued Israeli occupation and the adverse influence of the regional environment. Clear and realistic steps are needed, as well as sincere political will to undertake the necessary reform measures. Political progress in accordance with the Road Map and the honest implementation of their commitments by Israelis and Palestinians will ease the way toward successful Palestinian security sector reform (SSR).

However, many questions remain in this regard. Can the PNA security organisations fulfil their tasks of upholding law and order in the West Bank and Gaza, given their low capabilities and resources, especially in comparison with the armed Palestinian opposition? Which structural reforms are needed in the PNA security sector, and what kind of international assistance is required to implement these reforms? And how can international assistance be integrated into a medium- and long-term plan of SSR?

This chapter suggests some answers to these questions. It analyses the institutional and organisational shortcomings of the PNA security organisations, assesses the current SSR process on the Executive side – both on the level of management and the forces – and proposes some strategies for reform.[1]

A Performance Assessment of the PNA Security Organisations

Assessments of the PNA's performance in terms of security sector governance – and there have been a significant number since 1995 – do not differ much in their findings: the work of the PNA security organisations suffered from politicisation, strong personal loyalties, inflated personnel, overlap of tasks and responsibilities, a lack of inter-agency cooperation and a shortage of administrative skills. Weak judicial review and the lack of parliamentary monitoring compounded these problems. Moreover, Israel during the *Intifada* destroyed much of the Palestinians' security infrastructure and impeded the work of the security branches in a systematic manner.

These rather negative findings should not distract from a number of important achievements. Various organisations reached high levels of readiness and expertise in their areas of responsibility. The PNA security organisations up to 2000 also quite effectively dealt with crime and succeeded in maintaining more than just a modicum of stability in the areas under their control. Furthermore, before the *Intifada*, the security organisations quite effectively implemented their *Oslo* obligations to combat the infrastructure of extremist Palestinian organisations. What follows is a detailed performance and readiness assessment of the PNA security organisations.

Forces Structure

The biggest problem has been the absence of a central and unified command structure in many organisations such as *Preventive Security*, *General Intelligence* and *National Security Forces*. For instance, during Yasser Arafat's presidency, the Gaza and West Bank branches of the *National Security Forces* were put under the direct command of the President, but both had (and still have) different organisational structures. This resulted in different and at times incompatible internal regulations and operational procedures; another consequence was the increasing reluctance of the officers corps of both branches to cooperate. The absence of a central command structure – such as a 'general staff' – in the *National Security Forces* also resulted in the virtual autonomy of its administrative and operational departments, including the *Military Intelligence Department*, the *Training Department* and the *Political Guidance Department*. Furthermore, Arafat's refusal to enact a military retirement law led to a gerontocratic military leadership consisting of a large number of generals and colonels without actual functions. Needless to say, the Israeli reoccupation of the West Bank – including the destruction of security infrastructure, the confiscation of files and the arrest of personnel – and the physical separation of both parts of the homeland added significantly to the development of different organisational structures and cultures.

Tasks and Responsibilities

The divide and rule-policy of the late Arafat years and his refusal to endorse the creation of a legal framework for the security sector had a very negative impact on the delineation of tasks and responsibilities. Arafat created a set of parallel forces with identical functions and used to give one mission to different organisations which would then compete over its execution and over information and personal access to the President. Such conflict constellations included *Preventive Security* versus *General Intelligence*, *Preventive Security* versus *Special Forces*, *National Security Forces* versus *Military Intelligence*, *Presidential Security* versus *Presidential Guard*, *Presidential Security* versus *Naval Police*, and *Special Security* versus the so-called *External Security* in Tunis.[2]

Arafat's strategy and the turf wars in the security sector had grave consequences. Each security organisation maintained its own detention facilities which were beyond the realm of oversight. Various security commanders became active in business and illegal trading, such as the sale of confiscated vehicles and weapons on the black market. Extortion, illegal profiteering and unlawful arrests of citizens for ransom seriously discredited various organisations in the eyes of the public.

Human Resources Management

Weak human resources management has been another structural problem of the PNA security organisations. Firstly, the assignment of the limited number of specialised personnel – for example communications experts – to a whole range of different forces hampered the systematic application of their knowledge. Also, many security personnel were assigned duties that they had not been trained for; combat officers and soldiers of the *National Security Forces* were ordered to provide personal protection for PNA officials or to guard PLO offices; PLO air force personnel, including pilots and technicians, were employed in police functions and not in civil aviation, such as at Rafah airport.

Secondly, there has been no clear promotion policy. Some officers were dismissed or banned from taking higher positions on the basis of personal disputes, while others were promoted on the basis of loyalty rather than performance. This, coupled with the absence of financial or non-material incentives and low salaries in comparison with civil servants, has led to disappointment and mistrust among mid-level security officers in particular.

A third problem has been the large-scale recruitment of Fatah members into the security organisations. Although the majority of Fatah officials did not have any prior military or policing experience, they were given military ranks equal to the serving officers which caused considerable discontent. In various branches, this policy also led to the blurring of distinctions between military and political security work.

Fourthly, the PNA security organisations and especially the *Military Police* failed to enforce discipline among their members. In many cases, security officers used rank and file-personnel for private businesses or other non-security work; deserters were rarely persecuted, partly because they fled to areas under Israeli military control.

Israeli policies played a very negative role in addition to all of this. During the *Intifada* the Israeli army deported hundreds of specialised officers to Gaza, weakening the capabilities of the West Bank branches. Israeli closure policies severely limited the freedom of movement of security personnel, increased transportation costs and forced many officers to work in their towns or neighbourhoods of residence. This resulted in less security in the respective areas as security personnel were reluctant to enforce the law with regard to their kin and neighbours under the circumstances of armed conflict.

Training

The main training facilities for military, police and intelligence personnel are located in Gaza from where the majority of security officers originate. The physical separation of Gaza and the West Bank and the destruction of security infrastructure led to a decrease in the level of training and readiness in the West Bank. Except for the Police Academy in Jericho, at which the *Civil Police* are trained, there are no centralised training institutions for other organisations such as the *National Security Forces, General Intelligence* or *Preventive Security*. At the time of writing this article, the Intelligence Academy in Jericho was still awaiting completion. There are no unified and functional training curricula for security personnel, with Gaza and West Bank personnel of the same organisation receiving different training. In addition, Palestinian senior and mid-level officers graduated from a variety of international training institutions where they had been trained in different concepts of security, strategy, tactics and management, ranging from Western-style policing to Soviet military doctrines.

Motivation of Security Personnel

On the psychological level, the motivation of PNA security officers suffered significantly over the past four years. This is an important factor that has been often overlooked. Various factors have contributed to this development; systematic harassment, mistreatment and abuse of Palestinian officers by the Israeli army during incursions or at checkpoints being among the most important of them.

Security organisations were unable to protect their members when Israeli intelligence arrested them for investigation. They also failed to protect officers against revenge from family-and clan-networks, when an operation resulted in the arrest, injury or death of a person. Equally destructive of the morale of officers was the unwillingness to prosecute security commanders who had engaged in illegal activities and the lack of high-level political support for confronting armed Palestinian groups.

Inter-Agency Cooperation

Much has been said about the absence of effective mechanisms to ensure inter-agency cooperation and the resulting waste of resources and underperformance. On the most basic level, each security organisation operated on a separate communications network. Information was rarely shared at the command level. The exercise of joint operations rooms – established under the command of the *National Security Forces* in

2003 – remained ineffective due to limited willingness on the part of various commanders to cooperate.

On the political level, the National Security Council (NSC), officially revived by Arafat in 2002, was little more than a fig-leaf for the late President's continuing control over the security organisations and did not lead to the improved exchange of information. Later efforts by President Mahmoud Abbas to give the NSC real authority were half-hearted, and the failure of the PLC to agree on its mission and composition meant that there was never any legal basis for the body.

Finances

Vast differences exist with regard to the funding of the different organisations. The *National Security Forces* are under-funded in relation to their mission whereas other organisations such as the *Preventive Security* receive generous financial support, often directly from foreign donors. It goes without saying that this kind of funding is not mentioned in the annual budget of the organisations. Patronage networks within the agencies are another serious problem. Commanders have often bought the loyalty of their subordinates through cash bonuses which bear no relation to performance and operational achievements. Financial oversight by the government or the PLC has been negligent, because of both the absence of control mechanisms and a lack of political willingness. A striking example are the exorbitant expenses for the rent of infrastructure and housing, which are not properly accounted for.

Supply and Logistics

The security organisations suffer from the absence of clear and transparent procurement procedures. The 'General Procurement Authority' in the PNA has never managed to standardise supply mechanisms. The absence of an inventory control system has resulted in unnecessary and repetitive procurement. Purchases of equipment were made without thoroughly determining the needs of the organisations. Suppliers were determined on the basis of personal connections rather than cost-effectiveness, and many suppliers delivered goods and equipment of poor quality. Examples of mismanagement and corruption are legion: purchasing orders do not match received quantities; expenses for gasoline do not relate to the number of vehicles in the inventory; supplies are stolen and then resold into the private market.

Armament

The armament of the security organisations has been weak from the onset in terms of both quality and quantity. *Oslo II* allowed the PNA security agencies up to 4,000 rifles and 4,000 pistols, up to 120 machineguns of 0.3" or 0.5" calibre, and up to 15 light, unarmed riot vehicles in the West Bank; in Gaza, the Agreement allowed for 7,000 light personal weapons, up to 120 machineguns of 0.3" or 0.5" calibre, and up to 45 wheeled armoured vehicles. The current ratio of personnel to arms is four to one. Much of the armament was of poor quality – often Arab-made versions of Soviet small arms – and the quantities have never been sufficient for the number of personnel needing them. Security personnel also had to disassemble weapons in order to get spare parts, which were in short supply. Israeli military actions further depleted stocks. With some exceptions such as the *Civil Police,* there has been no proper inventory of weaponry. A lack of safe storage places or armouries prompted security personnel to take their weapons back home after duty.

Mobility

There has been no standardisation of the vehicle inventory. Different vehicles were used even within the same unit. The lack of four-wheel drive vehicles meant restricted mobility for many units, particularly in the hilly terrain of the West Bank. For many vehicles maintenance is difficult, either because they are old or because the local market does not supply spare parts for some types of cars. At the same time, many cars have large engines, consume large amounts of fuel and are thus not cost-effective. Another important problem is the lack of armour, especially for patrol and back-up vehicles, leaving personnel vulnerable to small-arms fire. Israeli military action destroyed many vehicles and in this way further contributed to reducing mobility.

Communications

The lack of reliable and secure communications systems is a major cause of operational underperformance. Palestinian forces have been using different and incompatible radio equipment, sometimes supplied and maintained by businessmen with personal connections to security commanders but with no or insufficient technical knowledge. Israel in 2003 destroyed many transponders and much of the other communications equipment.As a result, in late 2005, the West Bank and Gaza had radio coverage of only 25 per cent and no direct radio communication linking both areas. In the absence of other channels of communication, the PNA security forces have resorted to the use of the Israeli 'MIRS' communications network and the Palestinian mobile network 'Jawal'. Both are private systems and do not offer secure communications. Furthermore, the Israeli army has been obstructing the installation of antennas that would extend coverage.

On the other hand, poor communication is endemic in local culture. Vertical processing of information within the various organisations has been weak as has been horizontal information transfer between the different organisations. The transfer of orders from the command to the tactical level and vice versa has often been slow.

Oversight and Accountability

Under Arafat, there was no space for developing civil-democratic oversight or an accountability framework, given his direct control of the security sector. Neither the government, the PLC nor the Judiciary had any effective control over what happened in the security sector. A major factor was the absence of a comprehensive legal framework. Internal accountability too has been weak. The work of the Military Judiciary was subject to direct interference and manipulation by commanders and by Arafat himself. Moreover, many organisations had no internal control mechanisms at all; where control existed, as for example in the *Preventive Security*, it often lacked independence. Organisations also lacked standard procedures for dealing with disciplinary cases.

The SSR Process of 2005

After his election in early 2005, President Abbas made reforms in the security sector a policy priority. SSR was also seen as key by donor states, which sought to influence Palestinian security sector governance in many ways. However, they lacked vision and a clear reform strategy. Because of their inability to draw conclusions from previous experiences, progress was small and mostly limited to the reorganisation of command and control and some aspects of the rule of law. The security organisations were unable even to prevent attacks on the President's Office or the Minister of the Interior's residence.

SSR in the Palestinian context is no easy undertaking, partly because the PNA does not enjoy real authority over the territories under its jurisdiction, and partly because of insufficient governmental capacities and low government income.

The Palestinian economy is shattered and Palestinians, more than ever, depend on foreign assistance. Occupation leaves political, military and economic control in the hands of Israel and provides very little room for independent policy-making. In addition to that, there are also attempts by regional and international actors to impose their political agenda through the funding and armament of Palestinian militant groups. What follows is an assessment of the 2005 SSR process and the roles played by external actors in its course.

External Involvement in SSR

The Roles of Europe and Egypt: The beginning of the reform process can be dated back precisely to the 'London Meeting on Supporting the Palestinian Authority' which was held on 1 March 2005 under the auspices of the then British Prime Minister Tony Blair.[3] The London Meeting committed the PNA to a set of administrative, security and economic reforms. In the area of security, the PNA promised 'to create the conditions conducive to the peace process with the immediate objective of restoring internal law and order and preventing violence.'[4] More specifically, the PNA committed itself to embark on the creation of a legal framework for its security organisations and overhaul their command structure.

It was agreed in London that the Egyptian government would conduct a baseline-study of the PNA security sector in Gaza soon after the meeting. Based on this assessment, reform strategies and priorities were to be developed. The Egyptian government would also determine the material and training needs of the PNA security organisations. In March 2005, an Egyptian military adviser team under Lieutenant-General Mustafa Al-Behairy, the Deputy Commander of the Egyptian State Security Service

(Internal Intelligence), visited the Gaza Strip.[5] The team held a series of meetings with the Palestinian security leadership, namely the commanders of the different organisations and their deputies and planning officers, and assured them that they could rely on external support in reforming their agencies.

From the European side, the UK soon sent a liaison officer from the British army to work with the *National Security Forces*. In addition to that, Spanish and Canadian advisory teams were deployed to assess the *Civil Police* and the *Naval Police*. In April 2005, the Europeans set up a seven-strong UK-led European Coordination Office for Palestinian Police Support (EUCOPPS), which was tasked to assist the reform of the *Civil Police*. EUCOPPS managed to achieve some progress during 2005; an *EU-Palestinian Change Management Team for Civil Police Reform* was established, vehicles and riot-control equipment were delivered and police stations refurbished.

The US Role and SAI (Strategic Assessments Initiative): As the European and Egyptian missions began their work on the ground, the US Administration entered the scene and rushed to mark Palestinian security sector reform as its turf. In early February 2005, US Secretary of State Condoleezza Rice had announced that Washington planned to dispatch a high-level 'security coordinator' who would supervise the reform of the PNA security organisations.[6] In March 2005, Washington sent Lieutenant-General William Ward, then Deputy Commander of the US Army in Europe, with an US adviser team to the region and informed the PNA that the Ward Mission would be regarded as the only channel for international aid in security. Washington also pledged $3 million of assistance to the reform process. General Ward's mandate was later expanded to oversee the 'disengagement'-related security coordination between Israel and the PNA.

Once on the ground, the Ward Mission[7], composed of officials from the US Embassy in Tel Aviv, the US Consulate in Jerusalem and US military officers, established direct contact with the Palestinian security leadership in order to conduct a needs assessment. In practice, the US thereby overrode the Egyptian assessment process and limited the role of the Europeans strictly to *Civil Police* support. However, due to limited resources, lack of regional experience and the inability to send US personnel to Gaza[8], the Ward Mission soon decided to outsource the assessment function to a US-registered NGO called *Strategic Assessments Initiative (SAI)*. SAI marketed itself to Palestinians and donors as an 'independent third party' and had the advantage that security reforms would not have a purely US label.

SAI set up the International Transition Assistance Group (ITAG) in East Jerusalem, headed by the Canadian scholar Jarat Chopra. The ITAG team consisted of American-Palestinian consultants and retired military personnel from Germany, Italy, Canada and the UK; some of them were assigned by their national governments. ITAG had fairly good knowledge of Palestinian security sector governance, given that some of its consultants had previously worked for the PLO Negotiations Affairs Department (NAD); their knowledge of Arabic enabled them to establish good relations with the Palestinian security leadership. However, ITAG did lack real SSR expertise and had to compensate for this by recruiting personnel from *Control Risks*, a London-based risk-consultancy.

In April 2005, General Nasser Youssef, the Minister of the Interior and National Security, and General Ward agreed to establish a Palestinian-International Transitional Security Planning Team (TSPT). On the Palestinian side, the TSPT consisted of West Bank and Gaza representatives from the *National Security Forces*, *Civil Police*, *Preventive Security*, *Civil Defence* and *General Intelligence*; the Palestinian team was headed by Major-General Jamal Abu Zayed, then Assistant Minister of the Interior and National Security. The international side was represented by SAI and other international experts from Australia, Canada and South Africa. The TSPT was to focus on Israeli 'disengagement' from Gaza and parts of the northern West Bank and divided its work into two phases: In a first phase, a detailed capability assessment of the security sector would be undertaken, in order to determine the PNA's capacity to take over the evacuated areas and to ensure law and order in the post'disengagement' environment; this would also include security coordination with Israel. In a second phase, the TSPT would redesign the command and control structure in the Ministry of the Interior and National Security and coordinate the unification of the security organisations; the latter would include the practical unification process as well as the necessary training and material support to the various branches. An assessment of the military judiciary and the political oversight mechanisms was also intended.

In practice, the TSPT held around ten meetings in Gaza and the West Bank throughout spring and summer 2005. Discussions centred primarily on the planning for 'disengagement', the coordination between the security branches and the creation of joint operations rooms. Some consultants also made field visits to the *National Security Forces* in Gaza and Jenin in order to check their readiness before the Israeli redeployment began. Furthermore, the TSPT also attended two meetings with representatives from the donor community in Jericho in May and June 2005. The sessions, attended by General Youssef and General Ward, were meant to present the Palestinian planning for 'disengagement' and to gather further material and financial support.

However, the cooperation between the Palestinians[9] and the international side in the TSPT – especially ITAG – came to an abrupt end in July 2005 when SAI published its report 'Planning Considerations for International Involvement in the Palestinian Security Sector'. The report, which contained all the findings of ITAG's capability assessment, was leaked to several US newspapers and subsequently also appeared on the SAI website. The disclosure of the paper and its emphasis on corruption and lack of progress in reform, coupled with strong criticism of General Youssef, severely damaged the relations between the Palestinian representatives in the TSPT and ITAG. The Palestinians, who had hoped for sustained donor assistance based on ITAG's assessment, now saw all the problems in their security sector exposed to the world and felt betrayed, even more so because they had been told that the ITAG report would be confidential. Soon mutual accusations ensued between ITAG and General Ward on who was responsible for the leak. In late summer 2005, the Ward Mission then informed SAI that cooperation with ITAG would end after the Israeli 'disengagement.'

Lessons from External Involvement: ITAG's involvement in Palestinian SSR was in theory an appealing model: a non-state actor with local experience would serve as the go-between for Western state actors and help them overcome local legitimacy deficits.

In reality, however, the involvement of a private third-party proved a big failure. SAI was not only unable to convincingly communicate to donors the need for substantial material assistance to the PNA security organisations, it also discredited itself on the ground through its irresponsible public relations policy. In fact, all donor assistance delivered in 2005, as for instance the British and German support to the *National Security Forces*[10] or EUCOPPS's assistance to the *Civil Police*, occurred without any involvement of ITAG.

The role of US Security Coordinator Ward was also problematic. After defining Palestinian security as its turf in March 2005, in the following months Washington did surprisingly little to substantiate this claim. The Ward team focused almost solely on making the 'disengagement' work, and even here the few Palestinian-US meetings did not go further than reviewing the Palestinian concept of operations for the withdrawal. This was very much at the expense of actual long-term SSR. The weak impact of the US Security Coordinator was partly a function of the composition of the Ward team which consisted almost exclusively of US military personnel; these officers were taken out of their regular positions in Europe or elsewhere and assigned to work on Palestinian security at very short notice. The Ward team also lacked development expertise and funds. The US Security Coordinator did not even have a bank account or an infrastructure on the ground. Furthermore, General Ward himself was not permanently based in the region.

EUCOPPS played a more helpful role than Washington, especially in terms of material support. In Summer 2005, EUCOPPS delivered some 150 police vehicles as well as communications equipment to the *Civil Police* in Gaza and the West Bank, living up to the promises made by European officials earlier in the year. EUCOPPS also had the advantage of proximity to the Ministry of the Interior and National Security in Ramallah where it had an office; this allowed for constant contact with the Minister and senior security officials. However, the role of EUCOPPS has been limited to the *Civil Police* and did not extend to other security branches.

Reform Progress

Progress in PNA security reform has been slow and painful. Individual security commanders were reluctant to carry out orders from the political echelon and sometimes openly defied them when their personal interests where at stake.

Lower-ranking security personnel blocked streets or occupied public buildings, demanding a pay rise or protesting against what they deemed, sometimes rightly, unfair treatment by the security leadership. However, despite these obstacles the PNA made various reforms in 2005.

Rejuvenating the Security Leadership: In April 2005 President Abbas issued a decree ordering the retirement of various long-standing security commanders.[11]

Thereby a number of dominating figures in the security establishment were replaced with younger and supposedly more reform-minded officers.[12] The PNA in June 2005 also enacted the *Law of Service in the Palestinian Security Forces No. 8 of 2005* which limits the tenure of security commanders to a maximum of four years.[13]

Reorganising the Security Branches: Also in April 2005, Abbas ordered all PNA security organisations to merge into three branches – Internal Security Forces (Civil Police, Preventive Security, Civil Defence), National Security Forces (National Security Forces, Military Intelligence, Naval Police, Military Liaison, Presidential Security/Force 17), and General Intelligence – and to report to the Ministry of the Interior and National Security; this included General Intelligence which, although officially under the authority of the President, was simultaneously put under the Ministry in order to facilitate the reorganisation process.[14] Efforts were also made to enhance the implementation of Arafat's Presidential Decree Concerning the Attachment of Police, Preventive Security and Civil Defence to the Ministry of the Interior of 2002. The reorganisation of the security sector furthermore included the following steps:

- Dismantling of *Special Security*, a minor political security branch established by Arafat in the 1990s to supervise the other security organisations. Members of *Special Security* were assigned to the *National Security Forces*.
- Dismantling of the *Special Forces* which had been created by Arafat as a counterweight to the *Preventive Security* in the late 1990s (and were heavily supported by the British government in 2003 and 2004). Members of the agency, which had operational capacity only in the West Bank, were transferred to the *General Intelligence* and the *National Security Forces*.
- Efforts to enhance the integration of the *Presidential Guard Battalion* – responsible for the personal protection of President Abbas – under Brigadier-General Ghali Juma'a into the *Presidential Security* under Brigadier-General Faisal Abu Sharkh.
- Unification and standardisation of the Gaza and West Bank branches of the *Preventive Security* under the command of Major-General Rashid Abu Shbak.
- Merging of the different departments of the *National Security Forces* in the West Bank and Gaza, such as training, planning, transportation and logistics.
- Separation of the *Military Police* under Colonel Abed al-Rahim Abu al-Aoun from the *Military Intelligence* and integration of both organisations into the *National Security Forces* as separate departments. This also included the redefinition of responsibilities for both agencies.
- Division of the *Military Liaison* into two departments, the *Military Coordination* (which was made a department in the *National Security Forces* administration) and the *Joint Patrols* (which were merged with the *National Security Forces*); the *Military Liaison Department* includes the Palestinian elements in the Joint Security Committee (JSC) with Israel, the Regional Security Committees (RSCs) Gaza and West Bank, and the District Coordination Offices (DCOs).
- Reactivation/establishment of planning departments in the Ministry of the Interior and National Security and the various security branches.

Improving Human Resources Management: The most significant step in this regard was the creation of a military retirement system through specific laws[15] which require all security personnel above the age of 60 to resign. Resulting vacancies were filled with younger and more qualified officers. Some progress was made with the redistribution of security personnel according to their skills and specialisations. A clear and performance-based promotion scheme was introduced through the enactment of the *Law of Service in the Palestinian Security Forces No. 8 of 2005*; most important among the provisions in the law is the explicit prohibition of promotions based on personal contacts or kin affiliation. Furthermore, the Ministry of the Interior and National Security has increased the salaries of security personnel and put them on a par with the rest of the public sector.[16] Although salaries of security personnel are still very low by international standards, the pay rise has clearly boosted the morale of the rank and file.

Enhancing Training and Readiness: The PNA security organisations saw an improvement of training standards and readiness. Various training courses were held for *National Security Forces* officers without prior experience in military affairs, especially for those with a Fatah background. Courses at the *National Security Forces* training centres in Gaza and Jericho were opened for member of the *Al-Aqsa Martyrs Brigades*, with the first class of some 200 recruits graduating from Jericho in December 2005. Rehabilitation courses for security and police personnel were designed and partly implemented. Selected officers were sent for training to Algeria, Egypt, Jordan, Turkey, the UK and Yemen, although these numbers were small and did not match the training needs for higher and mid-level officers.

Reforming Financial Management: In an important step, the Ministry of the Interior and National Security in 2005 banned all PNA security organisations from receiving foreign aid through channels other than the Ministry itself. This measure put an end to the harmful practice of donors supporting individual agencies with funds and equipment, such as was the case with the UK and the US between 2000 and 2004; at the same time, the centralised disbursement of security aid through the Ministry also helped to curb patronage networks run by certain security commanders. Moreover, the PNA started to draft detailed budgets for the security branches in order to bring financial resources into line with tasks and missions; the Ministry of the Interior and National Security created an 'Oversight and Inspection Department' for auditing security expenditure.

Overhauling Logistics and Procurement: Throughout 2005 the PNA reviewed supply and procurement procedures in all security organisations. Procurement was centralised in the Ministry of the Interior and National Security and the issuing of tenders was made a requirement. A general inventory and maintenance check on weaponry was conducted in each branch; this included the scrapping of defective weaponry and the removal from inventory lists of all arms confiscated by Israel during the *Intifada*. In terms of vehicles, the PNA decided to purchase new cars only through the local Palestinian market. The respective suppliers (Mitsubishi and Land Rover for the *National Security Forces*, Volkswagen and Peugeot for the *Civil Police*, the latter financed by EUCOPPS) have adequate maintenance and repair facilities on the ground.

Rehabilitating the Communications Infrastructure: Communications networks of the security organisations were repaired as much as Palestinian capacities allowed for. The PNA bought large numbers of Israeli 'MIRS' devices; the branches directly involved in the 'disengagement' were also supplied with radio sets by the donor community. These are analogue devices and easy to eavesdrop but at least improved communications in the short term. EUCOPPS put significant effort into rebuilding the communications infrastructure and managed to establish almost full radio coverage for the *Civil Police* in Gaza and some 60 per cent coverage in the West Bank.

Creating a Normative-Legal Framework: Work on the creation of a legal framework for the security sector also yielded some success. Laws enacted by the PNA included the *Law of Service in the Palestinian Security Forces No. 8 of 2005*, the *Law of Insurance and Pensions for Palestinian Security Forces No. 16 of 2004*, and the *General Intelligence Law No. 17 of 2005*. In October 2005, the PNA also began work on a 'White Paper' in order to lay a conceptual basis for the PNA security sector, its structure and the direction of the future reform process.

Constraints on SSR

Throughout 2005, the PNA took some important steps to reform its security sector, in particular on an operational level and in relation to the legal framework. However, if the strategic and operational needs of the PNA security organisations are taken as the yardstick, this progress has been rather modest. In order to understand the mixed results in SSR and to devise a more realistic SSR strategy, one has to take into account a series of factors.

The Palestinian Domestic Environment: Internally, lack of progress in reform is to be attributed to a number of factors working on three different but interrelated levels: the PNA, the armed Palestinian factions, and the security organisations. On the PNA level, the reluctance to forcefully implement the 'Cairo Agreement' of March 2005 was problematic.[17] The Palestinian leadership never made any real efforts to establish the monopoly of force vis-à-vis the armed factions, even if those groups crossed the red line by killing PNA security officers.[18] Also the PNA neither prevented the rocket fire against Israel of the Islamic Jihad in Gaza[19] nor clamped down on criminal elements associated with the *Al-Aqsa Brigades*. By the same token it is also unclear to what extent the PNA leadership indeed backs the official merger of the security organisations into three branches.

Lack of political willingness for security reforms was compounded by an equal reluctance to combat corruption. Instead of persecuting individuals suspected of fraud or embezzlement, the PNA leadership transferred them to new posts, sometimes outside the country. Together with rampant nepotism and financing of armed groups through influential individuals in the PNA, this dealt a huge blow to the credibility and public legitimacy of the Authority.

On the level of the factions, the most serious security problems originate from the Fatah movement. Symptoms of Fatah's disintegration – infighting, assaults on rival politicians, attacks by militants on public property – abounded in 2005. In addition to that, some local branches of Fatah aligned themselves with regional powers for funding and political weight, in open defiance of the Fatah leadership and the PNA. At the same time, Hamas experienced a rapid political ascendancy, partly due to its military credentials, which culminated in its victory in the 2006 legislative elections. Also, the more important of the smaller Palestinian factions, such as the leftist PFLP (Popular Front for the Liberation of Palestine) and the Islamic Jihad, often side with Hamas.

The biggest problem on the organisational level is the dominant position of Fatah within the security sector. Almost all commanders and higher officers are members of Fatah. Its monopoly has resulted in a strong politicisation of the security establishment and the blurring of security and political work. Although politically a reasonable move, it is also not clear if the recruitment of – often unqualified – members of the *Al-Aqsa Brigades* into the security branches will contribute to the strengthening of capabilities.

Israeli Occupation: The policies pursued by the Israeli government and its army over the last six years are an equally big, if not bigger, obstacle to Palestinian SSR. In contrast to what some international observers had predicted, there was no political progress between Palestinians and Israelis after the 'disengagement'. On the contrary, Israel continued 'creating facts on the ground': the confiscation of Palestinian land, expansion of settlements in the West Bank, construction of the separation wall and demographic reengineering of Jerusalem. Thereby Israel helped undermine the political legitimacy of the PNA and indirectly supported Palestinian officials opposing SSR, who could argue that there was no need for an institutionalised Palestinian security sector under Israeli occupation.

Israel refused to implement the 'Sharm al-Sheikh Understanding' that was reached between the then Prime Minister Ariel Sharon and President Abbas in February 2006. The Understanding committed Israel to transfer security responsibility over the major West Bank cities back to the PNA, but in reality this never happened. The Israeli army continues to encircle Palestinian population centres through checkpoints and roadblocks and to invade them at will, regardless of their status under the *Oslo Agreements*. Israel also relentlessly pursued its policy of assassinations, triggering retaliation from militant groups and further destabilising the precarious security situation in the Palestinian Territories. Moreover, Israel repeatedly closed the Gaza crossing points for prolonged periods of time, leaving the Rafah crossing point as the only physical connection between Gaza and the outside world. Likewise, Israel refused to establish a safe passage between Gaza and the West Bank.

Israel also interferes with Palestinian capabilities at an operational level. It repeatedly vetoed the purchase of arms for reequipping the PNA security organisations and thwarted the supply of advanced communications equipment through EUCOPPS. The result is that militant groups such as Hamas' armed wing have better and more modern weaponry than the PNA; ironically the bulk of these arms originate from Israel and are purchased by armed groups on the black market. Israel also banned security personnel from travelling between Gaza and the West Bank and rejected Palestinian proposals to bring the *Badr Force* into the Palestinian Territories.[20]

Policies of Regional and International Actors: In general, regional and international actors did not play a helpful role for Palestinian SSR either. Iran, Syria and Hizbullah financially supported the Islamic Jihad and certain *Al-Aqsa* factions in order to advance their regional agenda. Egypt managed to facilitate the *tahdi'a* of March 2005 but failed to exercise its leverage with regard to a lasting Palestinian-Israeli ceasefire. Arab countries in general were very reluctant to support the Palestinian SSR process; only Saudi Arabia and the United Arab Emirates made major financial contributions which were however not specifically aimed at security reforms.

The US, clearly biased in favour of Israel and supportive of the Israeli paradigm of 'unilateralism', failed to pressure Israel to restart political negotiations after the 'disengagement', or even to coordinate its withdrawal with the PNA. The privatisation of the security file through SAI, lack of resources and a limited mandate precluded the US Security Coordinator from having any major impact in security reforms. At the same time, the US was unable or unwilling to bring in the international community to respond to the urgent needs of the nascent Palestinian SSR process.

Europe, which also bought into the illusion of 'disengagement', played a more helpful role, especially in relation to the *Civil Police*. However, this engagement is quite limited and at the expense of other security organisations which are in equally dire need of assistance and reform.

A Strategy for Palestinian Security Sector Reform

The Palestinian SSR process, even at its current embryonic stage, is a highly political endeavour. Its ups and downs are direct reflections of the political dynamics on the domestic scene and in the Palestinian-Israeli arena. Though short-term prospects are not bright, there is a chance for the Palestinian SSR process to succeed if Palestinians, Israelis and the international community undertake certain steps. Both parties need to respect their obligations under Phase I of the Road Map, Israel must respect the 'period of calm' (*tahdi'a*) and open a safe passage between Gaza and the West Bank, and the international community needs to help revive the Palestinian economy. In relation to Hamas' rise to power, Israel and the international community need to rethink their confrontational approach towards the new PNA government and find more constructive ways of engagement.

Successful SSR also requires sincere political will on the part of the Palestinian leadership, especially in relation to the unification of security branches and the prosecution of lawbreakers. This demands decisive steps to dismantle excessive power accumulation in the security sector and to reorient the organisational culture from personal towards institutional loyalty. What follows are some detailed recommendations for formulating a cohesive Palestinian SSR strategy. The recommendations focus on the role of the PNA Executive.

Reform Priorities

Activating the National Security Council (NSC): President Abbas' decree on reforming the NSC of September 2005 laid the groundwork for its reactivation but by summer 2006 nothing had happened. It is important that the NSC start its work. At the same time, its membership should be extended to include the Ministers of Information and Planning, the Chairman of the PLC Interior Committee, the Head of *General Intelligence*, the Chief-of-Staff of the *National Security Forces* and the Director-General of Internal Security.[21]

Reorganising Ministerial Control: Considering the obstacles to Palestinian SSR, it is unrealistic to expect that the Minister of the Interior and National Security alone will be able to push ahead the unification of branches and stop the security chaos. Reversing the trend of deteriorating security is the responsibility of all Palestinian institutions and political actors. Certain organisational steps could help enhance ministerial performance in this respect:

- The portfolios of the Interior and National Security should be divided and a separate Ministry of National Security be created. The latter should be in charge of the three PNA security branches and the reform process. This would give the Minister of National Security control of the Palestinian forces. The Ministry of the Interior would retain its current civilian departments only. An alternative option would be to put only *National Security Forces* under a specialised Ministry of National Security; the *Civil Police* as a law-enforcement agency would be kept under the Ministry of the Interior and be merged with a downsized *Preventive Security*.
- The security Minister(s) should have a military or security background and a strong personality. At the same time, he must not be affiliated to any power centres in the security branches.
- The Ministry of National Security should devise and implement a clear policy to coordinate the work of all security organisations. A modicum of coordination existed until April 2005, when security in Gaza and in the West Bank was under the command of two generals from the *National Security Forces*. However, since the retirement of the two officers, coordination between Gaza and the West Bank has collapsed. Despite what was reported in some media, there exists no central operations room for the three branches or inter-force operations rooms in the West Bank and Gaza.[22]
- The new Ministry would also need to decide whether human resource management should be assigned to a central department within the Ministry or left to each security organisation. The first option would be preferable.
- The new Ministry should also be given control over PLO military units deployed outside the country, as well as military attachés assigned to PLO embassies.

Pushing Ahead Reforms on the Forces Level: Reforms on the ministerial level would facilitate structural reforms on the forces level. Some forces still have a long way to go. For the *National Security Forces*, for instance, the following steps are required:

- The command structure and administrative management of the *National Security Forces* need to be reviewed, especially given that the headquarters and main installations of the organisation are still located in Gaza.

- The *National Security Forces* must improve communications between command centres in Gaza and the West Bank.
- The *Military Intelligence* must be effectively integrated into the *National Security Forces*. This also requires the unification of the West Bank and Gaza branches of the *Military Intelligence.*[23]
- The *Naval Police* should be divided into two different maritime units: A professional maritime component as part of the *National Security Forces*, which will lay the groundwork for a future PNA navy, and a maritime police unit under the *Civil Police* for combating smuggling. Personnel without maritime qualifications should be reassigned to other units of the *National Security Forces.*
- The *Presidential Security,* the so-called *Force 17*, should be integrated into the *National Security Forces*. The *Presidential Security* must have effective control over the *Presidential Guard Battalion.*

The three internal security agencies – *Civil Police, Preventive Security, Civil Defence* – should continue to operate under the supervision and control of the Ministry of the Interior. However, it is important that the *Internal Security Forces* become better coordinated. Plans to establish a joint command committee need to be implemented, and a Director-General for Internal Security must be appointed. As the integration of the *Preventive Security* into the *Civil Police* would have several advantages, it should be seriously considered.

Also, the separation of internal and external intelligence functions must be strictly implemented. Some progress was made with the enactment of the *General Intelligence Law No. 17 in 2005*, which defines external intelligence as the main remit of the organisation. However, the law gives the *General Intelligence* sweeping powers and thus contains many loopholes allowing for internal intelligence work. Many tasks of the *General Intelligence* continue to overlap with those of the *Preventive Security.*

All across the branches there is a need for professionalisation. The tentative retirement process started in April 2005 needs to be pushed ahead. Under-qualified personnel and those with criminal records must be dismissed and young qualified officers must be sponsored. As a matter of policy, security personnel should mainly serve in areas other than their hometowns. For speeding up the implementation of such a policy, the PNA should provide the necessary means of transportation or allocate allowances. Finally, cases of corruption involving senior or retired security personnel should be thoroughly investigated.

The Planning Process

Sound planning is a necessary precondition for successful Palestinian SSR. Planning must involve both the Ministries concerned and the forces.

Institutional Capacities: Planning capabilities at the Ministry of the Interior are weak. In order to strengthen them, the Ministry should set up without delay a planning and research department and appoint as its director a person who is qualified to take on strategic management responsibilities within the Ministry, possibly with the rank of Assistant Minister of Planning. In this capacity, the Director of the Planning and

Research Department would report directly to the Minister. He or she would also provide the National Security Council with relevant information, and steer and oversee planning activities within the three security organisations. A political decision to enhance planning capacity at the force level has been taken, but little has been done so far. Research and planning units should be established at the national command level of the three security organisations. The heads of these units should report directly to their respective force commanders and to the Planning and Research Department in the Ministry.

The planning unit of the *Internal Security Forces* should include representatives of all three internal organisations, and its head should preferably be recruited from the *Civil Police*. The units would undertake comprehensive planning for each security organisation.

Small planning and research units should also be set up at the regional command level of each organisation (West Bank and Gaza). The heads of these units would report directly to the head of the Planning and Research units of their respective force.

Planning Methodology: Regarding the design of the reform process it will be important to learn from the experience with the TSPT in summer 2005. An improvement of coordination among the Palestinian stakeholders in SSR is absolutely crucial. Before initiating the planning process, the Planning and Research Department in the Ministry should organise a series of workshops with the Minister and the core staff of the planning and research cells at the subordinate levels. The workshops must be based on a clear reform concept endorsed by the political leadership, preferably in the form of a provisional National Security Policy. On this basis, participants should then formulate the general methodology, objectives and benchmarks of the reform process.

Simultaneously, the Planning and Research Department, in cooperation with the Legal Department in the Ministry, should hold a series of workshops on the legal aspects of the reform process. This should be an inclusive endeavour that brings together the legal advisers of the security branches, representatives of the military judiciary, PLC members, representatives of civil society and academia, as well as international experts. The objective of these workshops would be to devise a strategy for strengthening civil-democratic oversight of the security sector. This strategy should be implemented in parallel with the reform measures of the Executive, so that decoupling the restructuring process from enhancing oversight and accountability will be avoided.

After the conclusion of these two workshop series, the Planning and Research Department would launch a third series of workshops with the heads of the three security branches, their planning cells and representatives of the military judiciary. Here the security leadership would approve the reform objectives and benchmarks on all levels, as well as a binding timetable for the reform process. Subsequently, the research and planning cells on the subordinate levels would translate the general reform strategy into concrete plans for their respective organisations. Inclusive workshops will be an important element in this regard.

International Involvement: Donors can play a helpful role in the planning process, provided that they are sincerely willing to support the Palestinian SSR. Notwithstanding negative experiences in the past, it would make sense for the US to take a lead in these efforts, given its vast resources and political clout. The US should put together a truly comprehensive and multidisciplinary international advisory team, including representatives from the US, Europe, Canada, Russia and Arab states such as Egypt and Jordan. Based upon Palestinian requests, the international team would provide advice and technical assistance to the planning process; it would also facilitate with Israel the movement of Palestinian security personnel and the import of equipment. Moreover, the international team would organise and facilitate regular security meetings between the Palestinian and the Israeli side. A special Palestinian team, led by the Head of the Planning and Research Department in the Ministry and composed of selected staff from the subordinate planning cells, would be the counterpart to the international team. However, given the negative experience with SAI in 2005, any new efforts to involve a private third party should be weighed very carefully.

Conclusion

The Palestinian security sector as a whole still suffers from grave problems, despite the progress achieved in 2005. This indicates that the factors accounting for the mediocre performance of the PNA security organisations run much deeper than ineffective command structures or lack of equipment and training. Dealing with the security legacy of the late Arafat, particularly the autonomous power centres in the security sector and the phenomenon of corruption and nepotism, will require sustained and long-term efforts by the Palestinians for which they need the help of the donor community. Reorganising the security branches with a view to a single and unified command structure will be a key precondition for all further reforms. However, in order to have a sustainable SSR process it is crucial equally that the restructuring at the forces-level be accompanied by commensurate reforms at the governance level, in particular the strengthening of parliamentary oversight and judicial review capacities.

It is hoped that this chapter, drawing on the reform experience of 2005, will provide some useful recommendations for future Palestinian SSR. The door is still open for the international community to play a helpful role in security sector reform and to support the Palestinians with the necessary political cover, expertise and hardware. At the end of the day, an efficient and democratically accountable PNA security sector is the only way to establish stability and order in the Palestinian Territories. It is also the only realistic way to enable the PNA to meet its obligations under the Road Map and thereby do its part on the way to peaceful coexistence with Israel.

Notes

1   This chapter is based on various interviews and numerous informal talks with Palestinian security personnel, as well as long-standing personal experience in the PNA and PLO security sector. Given the sensitivity of the topic, no indications concerning the sources of information are given in the following, except for information that is available to the public.

2   The *External Security* was created by Arafat in 1996 in order to coopt a former commander of the *Force 17*. The *External Security* functions more as a research centre than a security organisation, but it has a number of operatives that collect information in Europe and the Arab Middle East.

3   Originally, Blair had envisaged a political summit to reinvigorate the Road Map and lay the groundwork for renewed peace talks between Palestinians and Israelis. Thereby Blair had hoped to compensate for the dwindling US engagement in the 'peace process', symbolised by the withdrawal of US Special Envoy for Peace Talks John Wolf from the region in late 2004. Due to Israeli and US pressure, however, the UK government reformulated the scope and purpose of the summit: the gathering was to focus on PNA institutional and administrative reform instead of peace talks and would be called a mere 'meeting'.

4   *Conclusions of the London Meeting on Supporting the Palestinian Authority*, 1 March 2005, p. 6.

5   The Egyptian mission included 13 generals from various branches of the Egyptian armed forces, the Egyptian police and intelligence, and the Office of the National Security Adviser; the mission was expanded to 40 personnel in Summer 2005. In late 2005, Egypt also deployed mentoring teams to each of the 12 *National Security Forces* battalions in Gaza in order to improve the operational and leadership skills of their officer corps.

6   'Rice: US to appoint 'security coordinator', take more active role', AP, 7 Feb 2005.

7   General Ward left his post in November 2005 and was replaced by Lieutenant-General Keith Dayton, Director of Strategy, Plans and Policy at the Office of the Deputy Chief of Staff of the US Army. General Dayton previously served as Director of Operations for the US Defense Intelligence Agency (DIA) and Director of the Iraq Survey Group which engaged in the search for Iraqi weapons of mass destruction after the Iraq invasion.

8   Since the killing of three US security personnel in Beit Hanoun in the northern Gaza Strip in October 2003, US government personnel are not allowed to travel into Gaza for security reasons.

9   Notwithstanding the good working relations between ITAG and the Palestinian side, some duplication of work and confusion had already marked the assessment phase during Summer 2005.

10   The UK and Germany in spring and summer 2005 supplied the *National Security Forces* units in the Jenin District with communications devices.

11   *Presidential Decree on the Retirement of Security Personnel,* 22 April 2005.

12   Chief among them was Major-General Abd al-Razak al-Majaideh, Head of the *National Security Forces* in the West Bank and Gaza and nominal Commander-in-Chief of all PNA security organisations ('Head of Public Security'); his responsibility was taken over by the Minister of the Interior and National Security. Major-General Haj Ismail Jabr, Head of the *National Security Forces* in the West Bank, was replaced by Brigadier-General Nidal Asouli, former commander of the *National Security Forces* in Nablus. Brigadier-General Ahmad Arafat al-Qudwa, Head of the Military Administration, was replaced by Brigadier-General Mohammed Youssef. Brigadier-General Mahmoud Awad Allah, Director-General of Military Finance, was replaced by Brigadier-General Radwan al-Hillou. Furthermore, Major-General Moussa Arafat al-Qudwa, who had combined the posts of Head of *Military Intelligence* and the Gaza *National Security Forces*, was replaced by Brigadier-General Hisham Ibaid as Head of *Military Intelligence* and Brigadier-General Suleiman Hilles as Head of *National Security Forces* in Gaza (Moussa Arafat was killed by the *Nasser Salah ad-Din Brigades*, the armed wing of the Popular Resistance

Committees (PRC), in an assault on his Gaza home in September 2005). Major-General Amin al-Hindi, Head of *General Intelligence*, was replaced by Brigadier-General Tareq Rajab. Major-General Ala Hosni, the former Head of *Civil Police* in Bethlehem, replaced Major-General Saeb al-Ajez as Director of *Civil Police*. Major-General Ribhi Arafat, Head of *Military Liaison*, was replaced by Brigadier-General Samir Saksak. Finally, Brigadier-General Abu Youssef al-Wahidi, Head of *Special Security*, was sent into retirement.

13 *Law of Service in the Palestinian Security Forces No. 8 of 2005.*

14 *Presidential Decree Concerning the Unification of Security Forces,* 14 April 2005.

15 *Law of Insurance and Pensions for Palestinian Security Forces No. 16 of 2004; Public Retirement Law No. 8 of 2005.*

16 *Decision of the Council of Ministers Concerning the Raising of the Salaries of the Military Personnel,* 8 September 2005.

17 The 'Cairo Agreement' of 16 March 2005 was concluded between the PNA, Hamas, Islamic Jihad and 11 smaller factions and committed all groups to a *tahdi'a* or 'period of calm' vis-àvis Israel.

18 For example, in March 2005 Hamas operatives shot and killed the Head of *Civil Police* in the Sha'ati Camp in Gaza City.

19 A case in point were the assaults by Fatah militants on various restaurants in Ramallah in April 2005, after they had been expelled from the Presidential Compound. In the aftermath of the incident, the *National Security Forces* Commander of Ramallah was fired for his failure to protect public property, but the assailants, albeit well-known, were never prosecuted. This was even more surprising because they also opened fire on the Presidential Compound.

20 The *Badr Force* is a 2,000-strong PLO military unit deployed in Jordan. The *Badr Force* was trained by the Jordanian army and police and was envisaged to help establishing law and order in the post-'disengagement' environment.

21 Currently, the NSC comprises the President, the Prime Minister, the Ministers of the Interior, Foreign Affairs, Civil Affairs and Finance, the National Security Adviser, and the Head of the PLO Negotiations Department.

22 The misunderstanding seems to go back to a UK initiative of 2004 to establish two antiterrorist operations centres in Gaza and the West Bank. These however never became functional.

23 The danger of a 'hostile takeover' of the *Military Intelligence* by personnel from the disbanded *Special Forces* seems to have been averted since the commander of the *Special Forces* was killed in the Amman bombings of 9 November 2005.

Civil-Democratic Oversight of the PNA Security Sector

Majed Arouri and Mamoun Attili

Each country has a range of security organisations, which protect the state and its citizens from internal and external threats. The structure of the security sector may differ from one political model to another. However, a central feature of civil-democratic security sector governance is that the security organisations abide by the laws and rules issued by democratically-elected representatives and are accountable for their activities. In other words, in democratic countries security organisations aim both to protect the elected political leadership and to ensure the security and safety of the citizens.

Security organisations are invested with certain prerogatives and powers for the sole purpose of protecting the rights of the citizens and the democratic system; consequently, in a functioning democracy, oversight mechanisms are put in place to monitor the security organisations and their performance. Oversight applies to all areas of activities: the collection of information (intelligence), the repression of criminal acts (law enforcement) or the use of military force (defence). Effective oversight protects the political institutions and the citizens from the abuse of power by police, army or intelligence. A central feature of oversight is to ensure the accountability of the security sector to the Legislature and Judiciary.

This chapter describes the systems for the Palestinian oversight of security organisations, including the Palestinian Legislative Council (PLC), the Judiciary and Palestinian civil society with its various components. It also makes some recommendations on how to improve the PNA oversight capacity as part of a wider reform process of the Palestinian political system.

Parliamentary Oversight

It is important to keep in mind that the Palestinian political and legal system is still under construction. Only some ten years have passed since the creation of the PNA and its institutions. Notwithstanding the difficulties involved in the state-formation process, Palestinian institution-building has the chance to benefit from previous international experiences in the field of political and legal development. The PLC as the elected representative body of the Palestinian people has a variety of tools to oversee the performance of the Executive and its security branches.

Legal Basis for Parliamentary Oversight

The legal basis of the Palestinian governance system is the *Amended Basic Law of 2003*. Its *Article 5* states the following:

'The governing system in Palestine shall be a democratic parliamentary system based on political and party pluralism. The President of the National Authority shall be directly elected by the people. The Government shall be responsible before the President and the Palestinian Legislative Council.'

In addition to that, *Article 47 (1)* of the *Amended Basic Law* states that the PLC is the elected legislative authority. In combination, these norms provide the legal foundation for the PLC and its activities. The *Amended Basic Law* also contains specific provisions regarding the oversight instruments that the PLC has at its disposal. Further regulations are included in the *Standing Orders*, the PLC bylaw of 2003.

Oversight Instruments

The *Amended Basic Law* stipulates in *Article 74* that the PNA government is accountable to the PLC:

'1 The Prime Minister is accountable to the President of the National Authority for his actions and the actions of his government.
2 Ministers are accountable to the Prime Minister, each within the limits of their jurisdiction and for the actions of their respective ministry.
3 The Prime Minister and members of the government are jointly and individually accountable to the Legislative Council.'

In order to ensure this, the Legislative Council can resort to a series of oversight instruments.

Inquiries, Interpellations and Hearings: The main instruments for individual PLC members to exercise oversight are inquiries, interpellations and hearings. *Article 56 (3)* gives every PLC member the right to *'address inquiries and interpellations to the government, to any minister or to those of equal rank.'* [1]

Inquiries are to be specific and must be submitted in writing to the PLC Speaker.[2]

The PLC can only discuss the matter under question seven days after the submission of an inquiry. The exception are cases where a government official is willing to respond within a shorter timeframe. Furthermore, if the matter of an inquiry is of special urgency, the seven-day period may be shortened to three days with the approval of the PNA President.[3]

In procedural terms, an inquiry is transferred by the PLC Speaker to the government and put on the agenda of the subsequent session of the Council; unless decided otherwise, the PLC will devote the first 30 minutes of this session to the inquiry.[4] In the course of the debate, Council members have the right to ask complementary questions.[5] The government member under inquiry may ask to postpone his response to the following PLC session, unless the inquiry is adopted under urgency procedures which requires him to respond immediately.[6]

Interpellations are inquiries coupled with a no-confidence vote. *Article 57 (1)* of the *Amended Basic Law* gives a minimum of ten PLC members the right to request the withdrawal of confidence from the government or a minister upon completion of an inquiry. Voting on such a request may not be held earlier then three days after submission. A no-confidence vote requires the approval of the absolute majority of PLC members.[7] In procedural terms, interpellations function like inquiries, with the exception that parliamentarians submitting an interpellation are required to explain to the Council its objective.[8]

Hearings are somewhat different from inquiries and interpellations in that they are not explicitly mentioned in the law. The PLC derives the right to hold hearings with members of the Executive from *Article 56* of the *Amended Basic Law* which states that every PLC member has the right to '*to submit to the Executive branch all legitimate requests necessary to (...) carry out parliamentary functions.*' Furthermore, *Article 57* of the *Standing Orders* says that the PLC committees '*(...) may request any minister or responsible person in the PNA to give information on or clarify any point related to the subjects referred to it or which lie within its scope.*' Hearings are held to summon ministers, civil servants or security officials for questioning on a specific matter.

There is also another important difference between inquiries, interpellations and hearings: inquiries and interpellations can only be directed at the government and its members who are directly accountable to the PLC. In addition to that, hearing requests may also be directed at the PNA President and security officials under his control who are not accountable to the PLC according to the *Amended Basic Law*.

Fact-Finding Committees: The PLC may form fact-finding committees in order to gather information on specific issues. *Article 58* of the *Amended Basic Law* states that such committees can be established '*regarding any public matter or (...) any public institution.*' *Article 48 (3)* of the *Standing Orders (2003)* confirms this right, adding that ad-hoc committees may '*fulfil temporary or permanent purposes and specific objectives.*' The PLC may also delegate fact-finding to one of its regular committees, such as the Committee for Oversight on Human Rights and Public Freedoms or the Interior and Security Committee.

Votes of No-Confidence: In addition to interpellations, there are two more types of no-confidence vote in the *Basic Law*. The first is a vote of confidence held in conjunction with the formation of the government: after the nomination of the Council of Ministers, the PNA Prime Minister is required to ask the PLC for a special session in order to obtain parliamentary confidence.[9] The Prime Minister has to lay out the programme and planned policies of his government upon which a parliamentary debate is held; this must take place within one week of the Prime Minister's request.[10] The PLC votes collectively on the government unless parliamentarians have decided otherwise by absolute majority.[11] *Article 66 (3)* of the *Amended Basic Law* requires an absolute majority for the vote of confidence.

The second type is by Article 77 of the Amended Basic Law (2003) which states in Paragraph 1 that 'a minimum of ten Members of the Legislative Council may submit a request to the Speaker to hold a special session to withdraw confidence from the government or from any minister after an investigation.'[12] The voting session shall be fixed three days after submission of the request and not more than two weeks later.[13] A vote of no-confidence requires the absolute majority of parliamentarians.[14] If the

PLC withdraws confidence from the Prime Minister or the government, the PNA President needs to appoint a new Prime Minister within two weeks.[15] If the Council withdraws confidence from an individual minister, the Prime Minister is required to present a new minister to the PLC within two weeks.[16]

Complaints: Beside the above-mentioned instruments, there is also a complaints function in the PLC. This is however not stated in the *Basic Law* but in the *Standing Orders*. According to *Article 100* of the *Standing Orders (2003)*, '*every Palestinian citizen has the right to submit a complaint concerning public affairs*' to the Council. Such a complaint must be signed and include name, profession and address of the petitioner or the petitioning legal entity. The PLC Speaker forwards these complaints to the Oversight Committee or any another committee under whose remit the complaint falls.[17] In this process, the Oversight Committee functions as a clearing house and refers complaints either directly to the government or another more specialised committee.[18] The Speaker may drop complaints that do not comply with formal requirements.

Oversight Performance of the PLC

As shown above, the PLC has quite a variety of oversight tools at its disposal, very much like other parliaments around the world. However, the best legal framework is of limited value if not implemented in practice. It is therefore important to take a look at how the PLC has actually performed in overseeing the PNA security organisations over the past years. Two phases can be distinguished here.

Institutional Paralysis (1996 – 2004): In the period from the establishment of the PLC in early 1996 until the death of Arafat in November 2004 the Council exerted rather limited oversight. This period was characterised by a slow and painful process of institution-building, marked by 'trial and error.' Power struggles among political actors dominated the relations between the Executive, the PLC and the Judiciary. Different political visions of how the PNA should function institutionally exacerbated these tensions. The PNA institutions evolved in the room which they were given by the President and his advisers, rather than the law. As a result, the PLC made hardly any effective use of its oversight authority. For example, the PLC only held five inquiries on security matters between 1996 and 2004, all of them before the outbreak of the *Intifada*; also votes of no-confidence were never used in practice.

The lacklustre oversight performance of the Legislative Council also had other reasons. Being created from scratch, the PLC simply lacked the experience and knowledge of parliamentary work. There was also no effective opposition in the Council, which was dominated by one political party, namely Fatah. In addition, the PLC could hardly be considered an independent institution in terms of separation of powers. A large number of its members held positions in the government; many representatives were personally close to Arafat and subject to his influence which became evident in voting patterns. Often Council members would not adhere to the procedures stated in the *Basic Law* and the *Standing Orders*. Outspoken PLC members were physically assaulted by security personnel; the failure of the Council to take any decisive steps against such attacks harmed the public image of the PLC and led to the silencing of many critics of the Executive.[19] Finally, until 2002 Arafat himself held the posts of Minister of the Interior and Commander-in-Chief of the Armed Forces which legally put all Palestinian security organisations under his direct authority and supervision. Thus, even if the PLC had been willing to question Arafat on security matters, it would have hardly been able to do so due to the lack of clear legal mechanisms for questioning the PNA President.

Increased Activity (since 2004): The situation in the PLC changed significantly after November 2004. Following Arafat's death, PLC Speaker Rawhi Fattouh took over the PNA Presidency *ad interim*. During this period and even more so after the election of Mahmoud Abbas in January 2005, the PLC began to live up to its legislative and monitoring responsibilities for the first time. There were various indicators for this institutional recovery. In 2005, the PLC threatened to hold a no-confidence vote against the government in the context of the deteriorating security situation. Also, Council members increasingly insisted on working according to the procedures stated in law, both internally and in relation to the Executive and Judiciary. There has also been more insistence on formally accepting draft laws submitted by the Council of Ministers.

Although the Council's more active role did not translate into equally ambitious oversight of the security sector – precisely because the majority of members belonged to the same party as the security leadership – the PLC has undertaken encouraging steps in this direction too. In 2004 and 2005, the Oversight Committee held some ten hearings with government members and security commanders. In April 2005, 16 PLC members published a memorandum calling for an inquiry into a series of grave security incidents in Ramallah. The Oversight Committee in May 2005 also issued a scathing report on the security situation in the Palestinian Territories, blaming the government openly for its failure to uphold law and order. As this report is the first comprehensive output of the PLC in terms of security oversight, it merits a closer look.

The 'Report on the Security Situation in the Palestinian Territories (May 2005)' was based on the findings of a fact-finding mission conducted by the Oversight Committee on the deterioration of the internal security situation in the Palestinian Territories (see Appendix B). The investigation focused particularly on the performance of the PNA security organisations and the Ministry of the Interior and National Security. The report, unusually candid in its language, contained the following conclusions:

- The PNA's lack of willingness to establish law and order led to a significant increase in killings, assaults and misuse of firearms in the Palestinian Territories. This encouraged Palestinian citizens to take the law into their own hands. Furthermore, individuals with political or business 'connections' encourage criminal acts and interfere with the Judiciary.
- There is no coordination between the PNA security organisations. Instead, competition between the different branches is high; this includes armed confrontations between members of the different organisations. The *Presidential Decree Concerning the Unification of Security Forces of 14 April 2005* was not implemented in practice.

- The PNAsecurity organisations are unable or unwilling to prosecute those responsible for breaking the law. Therefore the security commanders are directly responsible for the deteriorating security situation.
- Many criminal activities are perpetrated or instigated by security personnel or members of political parties. Therefore the PNA, Fatah and the security leadership bear direct responsibility for the security chaos.
- Although aware of the security chaos, the Ministry of the Interior and National Security failed to take any effective measures to improve the security situation. Financial and administrative mismanagement in the Ministry undermines the performance of the security organisations.
- The Minister of the Interior and National Security communicates directly with the security branches on various levels, thereby bypassing security commanders and violating the chain of command. This undermines the performance of the security agencies and endangers their organisational cohesion.
- The annual security budget is insufficient and the mechanisms for the distribution of funds between the different security organisations are unclear.

The report called upon the PNA Executive to take steps against the security chaos and demanded that security commanders assume personal responsibility for the failure of their branches. The Minister of the Interior and National Security was summoned to improve the work of all agencies, establish effective security coordination mechanisms and present the PLC with a draft legal framework for the whole security sector. The report also demanded the Executive stop interfering with the Judiciary, in particular regarding the implementation of court decisions. The Judiciary was summoned to reorganise itself and improve its performance under the proviso of judicial independence.

As a follow-up to the report, the PLC in June 2005 held a hearing session with the then Minister of the Interior and National Security, General Nasser Youssef, and asked him to explain which measures had been taken by the Ministry to restore law and order. The Minister stated that he had made efforts to merge the security organisations and that 60 per cent of the unification benchmarks had been met. The Ministry had also started to implement a security plan[20] in the areas under its control. Interestingly, the Minister openly stated that he lacked the necessary resources and political backing for his work. PLC members sharply criticised the performance of the Minister and his response to the Council, underlining that no real improvement of the security situation had taken place.[21]

Up to the end of 2005, the practical impact of the PLC's new oversight activity unfortunately remained weak, although the PLC Interior Committee undertook further investigations of the security reform process. A resolution issued by the Council in June 2005, calling on the then Prime Minister Ahmad Qurei to put an end to the security chaos, remained without effect, although supported by 44 of the 88 PLC members.[22] Yet, the end of the Arafat-era and the outcome of the January 2006 PLC elections without doubt provide an opportunity to enhance parliamentary oversight in the Palestinian Territories. The PLC instruments might not be perfect but past experiences in sectors other than security have shown that they can be effective if properly applied. Increased political diversity in the Council and the existence of a strong opposition may very well inject some momentum in this regard. In addition, current efforts to build a legal framework for security give the PLC the chance to insert a civil-democratic vision into PNA security sector governance.

Judicial Review

The vast powers of the PNA security branches necessitates that they are accountable to the Judiciary. This refers in particular to the use of force and all other actions which might infringe on the rights and freedoms of the Palestinian citizenry. In other words, the principle of judicial review in relation to the security organisations is a key element of the rule of law.

Legal Framework

Judicial oversight over the security sector is not directly regulated in the *Basic Law*, but it gives every Palestinian the right '*to submit a case to court (...) and to seek redress in the judicial system.*'[23] Except for this provision, references to judicial review are rather sparse in the *Amended Basic Law. Articles 101103* stipulate the establishment of military, administrative and constitutional courts but say nothing about their competencies. *Article 107* establishes the PNA Attorney-General and *Article 106* states that '*(...) obstructing the implementation of a judicial ruling (...) shall be considered a crime carrying a penalty of imprisonment or dismissal from position.*'

Rather than in the *Basic Law*, the legal framework for judicial review of the security sector and its activities is enshrined in simple legislation: the *Law of the Formation of Regular Courts No. 5 of 2001,* the *Law of the Judicial Authority No. 1 of 2002* (a version amended in 2005 awaits final approval) and the *Penal Procedure Law No. 3 of 2001*. It is especially the latter text which states that the PNA security branches are to operate under the rule of law. *Articles 20* and *21* of the *Penal Procedure Law No. 3 of 2001* require the PNA Attorney-General to oversee the work of law-enforcement personnel and to take disciplinary action if they fail to comply with the procedures stated in law. *Articles 29* and *39* of the same law ban unlawful arrests and house searches without warrant. The *Law of the Formation of Regular Courts No. 5 of 2001* in *Articles 33* and *34* gives citizens the right to file a complaint to the PNA High Court against unlawful arrests or other administrative acts of the security branches; any unlawful administrative act can be annulled by the High Court.

Judicial Review in Practice

To its credit, the PNA Judiciary in the past made serious efforts to monitor the work of the security organisations. In particular complaints to the High Court have proven an effective instrument: in recent years, the Court abolished some 100 detention orders issued by the security branches or lower courts which had resulted in unlawful arrests.[24] Administrative courts have taken similar decisions on various occasions. Complaints with the High Court also helped to identify those security organisations which were especially at risk of engaging in unlawful activities such as the *Preventive Security* and the *Military Intelligence.*[25]

In sum, however, judicial review of the security sector was weak in its extent and effectiveness. Neither the courts nor the Attorney-General were able to effectively oversee the activities of the security organisations and to protect the rights of the citizens. On the contrary, the Judiciary often had to defend itself from interference by the political echelon or the security establishment. As with the Legislature, the problem here is not so much the absence of a legal framework. Although there is arguably room for improvement, the legal basis for effective judicial review is actually in place; past activity of the courts shows that if willing, the PNA Judiciary can make successful use of the available instruments. As is the case with other elements of the security sector, the main reasons for the meagre judicial performance are political: many judges and officials in the prosecution are members of Fatah. This has resulted in a culture of clientelism, with appointments and promotions based on personal relations and political affiliations rather than upon merit and qualification.

Given that the security branches are also dominated by Fatah there is little willingness to prosecute security officials involved in unlawful activities. In addition to that, the Executive on many occasions directly interfered with the courts; the security branches have regularly disregarded court orders or delayed their implementation.[26]

The Role of Palestinian Civil Society

The unique Palestinian political and social context has enabled the development of a strong civil society, especially when compared to other Arab states. Long-standing grass roots activism and the experience of the first *Intifada* resulted in a tradition of freedom of speech, civil protest and political criticism.

Palestinian NGOs and the Security Sector

After 1994, Palestinian civil society organisations and human rights groups increasingly began to monitor the activities of the PNA, in addition to the Israeli occupation authorities. This meant parallel work: on the one hand, Palestinian NGOs continued to document Israeli violations of Palestinian human rights in order to expose them to the international community; on the other hand, these groups documented and followed-up human rights-violations by the PNA security organisations, in particular assaults on public demonstrations, infringements on the freedom of speech, unlawful arrests and house searches and the abuse of prisoners.

In terms of their approach, Palestinian NGOs have been focusing on public awareness and solidarity campaigns, in order to pressure the PNA to comply with international human rights standards. Some NGOs have also begun to represent civilians in courts and achieved the cancellation of court orders and the release of unlawful detainees. Civil society organisations furthermore use reports and press releases to expose violations of citizens' rights. Many Palestinian NGOs issue periodical publications on the security conditions in the Palestinian Territories which often give a more accurate picture of the situation than the Palestinian press. Civil society organisations that monitor the activities of the security organisations include the Palestinian Independent Commission for Citizens' Rights (PICCR), *Al Haq* – Law in the Service of Man, the Treatment and Rehabilitation Center for Victims of Torture (TRCT), the *Al-Mezan* Center for Human Rights and the Palestinian Center for Human Rights.[27] Some recent examples illustrate the activities of Palestinian civil society and the range of actors involved:

- In June 2005, members of the National and Islamic Factions, an umbrella group founded at the onset of the second *Intifada*, threatened to organise a campaign of civil disobedience in Ramallah if the PNA Executive did not take effective steps against the security chaos in the Palestinian Territories. Representatives of the group demanded the resignation of the President and the government. At the same time, the Palestinian Bar Association declared a one-day strike in solidarity with the demands of the National and Islamic Factions.
- Civil society organisations played a crucial role in monitoring the activities of security personnel during the Palestinian elections of 2005 and 2006.[28] Various NGOs dispatched observers who recorded violations by security personnel, such as the failure to implement the ban on arms in electoral offices or the display and firing of weapons during election rallies.
- In an unprecedented move, a lawyer from Ramallah in June 2005 filed a lawsuit against President Abbas, Prime Minister Qurei and PLC Speaker Rawhi Fattouh. Citing *Article 30 (1) Amended Basic Law (2003)*[29], he accused them of direct responsibility for the anarchy and security chaos in the areas under PNA control. A decision of the High Court in this matter was pending, at the time this chapter was written.

However, despite these and many other successful activities, Palestinian civil society has not been able to exercise effective oversight over the PNA security forces. Palestinian NGOs play a very important role in Palestinian politics, but it is obvious that they lack the capacity and political clout to compensate for the failure of Executive, PLC and Judiciary in terms of oversight.

The PNA Ombudsman

Since its establishment in 1993, the Palestinian Independent Commission for Citizens' Rights (PICCR) has made an important contribution to improving civil-democratic oversight in the PNA areas. The PICCR is called for in *Article 31 Amended Basic Law (2003)*[30] and was established by presidential decree. Although it is technically not an NGO, the PICCR has often played the role of opposition vis-à-vis the PNA. The PICCR has the twin function of PNA ombudsman and national human rights institution. Although its powers are not yet regulated by law – the drafting of respective legislation has been under way – the PICCR managed to develop rather effective working mechanisms, based on the powers contained in the presidential decree and its internal bylaw. The PICCR has also managed to build good relations with the PNA institutions over the last ten years.

The PICCR has the mandate to investigate and document human rights violations by the PNA security organisations on the basis of complaints received from the citizens. The Commission checks the complaints in terms of contents and investigates with the concerned institutions and organisations. The PICCR particularly tries to ensure that the security branches abide by the law when conducting house searches, arrests and detentions; moreover, the Commission works to prevent the use of torture during interrogations.

The PICCR made an important contribution to the development of a civil society 'monitoring culture' through awareness campaigns, regular visits to security installations and human-rights training of security personnel. Gradual improvements in the human-rights record of the security organisations[31] show that persistent efforts by civil society can make an impact. However, the PICCR still lacks the instruments to enforce access to information in cases where the PNA is unwilling to cooperate. In its work, the Commission is thus mostly still dependent on the goodwill of security commanders and PNA officials.

Conclusions and Recommendations

Taking into account the difficult security environment in the Palestinian Territories and the low degree of institutionalisation in the PNA, one can conclude the following for the oversight performance of the Legislature and Judiciary and the role of civil society:

- Under the tenure of the late President Arafat parliamentary oversight over the PNA security organisations was weak. Executive and partly also legislative powers were concentrated in Arafat's hand, dwarfing the role of the PLC in all sectors including security. Arafat's authoritarian rule, personal overlap between the PLC and the government, and the uniform political composition of the Legislature made the PLC unfit for effective oversight.
- Since the beginning of 2005 a slight improvement in parliamentary oversight could be noted. Security-related reporting and questioning through the PLC appeared. The merging of security organisations under the Ministry of the Interior and National Security created a single political address that could be held accountable, even though the unification was not fully implemented in reality.
- The Judiciary has long underperformed in terms of review. Although a legal framework exists to hold the security personnel accountable through the courts, political interference, factional loyalties and lack of capacity have yielded practical review ineffective.

- Palestinian civil society organisations have not been able to make up for the lack of effective oversight on part of the PLC and the Judiciary, notwithstanding serious efforts of monitoring and campaigning by human rights NGOs.

In order to improve civil-democratic oversight in the PNA in a sustainable fashion, a comprehensive approach is needed which involves the PLC, the Judiciary and civil society at the same time. Parallel reform steps must be taken in all three sectors:

- The PLC has to effectively assume its oversight responsibility in relation to the Executive and the security organisations specifically. The Palestinian legislative elections of January 2006 have brought a rejuvenated and more diverse Legislative Council; this provides a tremendous opportunity for strengthening its performance.
- To this effect, the PLC should make real use of all parliamentary instruments and, where necessary, improve the legal framework for oversight. The PLC should also work to build an effective working relationship with the government; this would include establishing clear and agreed procedures for accessing security-related information. The Council must also be enabled to effectively oversee all financial matters pertaining to the security sector, especially the budgets of the various agencies. This will require further work on establishing a sound legal framework for the security sector. Finally, the PLC must reform its own administrative structure and receive the necessary resources in terms of personnel, infrastructure, and knowledge-management.
- The Judiciary, including all its subsidiary branches, must be enabled to oversee interrogation and detention centres as well as prisons which are currently subordinate to various security branches. The security agencies must be compelled to respect court decisions, in particular those annulling administrative acts. It is also important that the Public Prosecution investigate and act against any practices of administrative detention without court orders.
- Civil society organisations must make joint efforts to put an end to illegal practices in the security sector, foremost among them illegal detention and torture. Palestinian and international media, public awareness campaigns and public demonstrations have to be used more systematically. Also, political parties and the media themselves must play a more active role in overseeing the work of the security organisations. Finally, there is an urgent need to create space for a public debate on security sector governance and what security should mean for the Palestinian citizens.

Notes

1   This provision in the *Basic Law* is not very clear. The last part can be translated as either 'of equal rank' or 'under his authority', with rather different results in terms of whether the PLC is entitled to summon government officials below the rank of minister.
2   *Standing Orders (2003), Article 75 (2).*
3   *Amended Basic Law (2003), Article 56 (3).* In addition to this, *Article 81 Standing Orders (2003)* gives the PLC the right to adopt a so-called urgency procedure upon a written request by five PLC members or a parliamentary committee. *Article 82 Standing Orders* states that matters adopted under emergency procedures must be dealt with before all other issues on the PLC agenda and that there are no time limits to discuss them.
4   *Standing Orders (2003), Article 77.*
5   Ibid., *Article 78.*
6   Ibid., *Article 77.*
7   *Amended Basic Law (2003), Article 57 (1).*
8   *Standing Orders (2003), Article 80 (4).*
9   *Amended Basic Law (2003), Article 66 (1).*
10 Ibid., *Article 66 (1).*
11 Ibid., *Article 66 (2).*
12 The provisions of *Article 77* regarding the motion of confidence do not substantially differ from the interpellation of *Article 57*. In the course of future changes of the *Basic Law* the two articles could be combined into one.
13 *Amended Basic Law (2003), Article 77 (2).*
14 Ibid., *Article 78 (1).*
15 Ibid., *Article 79 (1).*
16 Ibid., *Article 79 (2).*
17 *Standing Orders (2003), Article 102 (1).*
18 Ibid., *Article 102 (2).*
19 Palestinian Independent Commission for Citizens' Rights (PICCR), *The Status of the Palestinian Citizens' Rights during 2004. The Tenth Annual Report*, Ramallah 2005, p. 37.
20 The security plan, according to the Minister, included campaigns in Gaza and various cities in the West Bank to stop assaults on public institutions, confiscate stolen vehicles and combat drug-trafficking.
21 The Minister made some remarkably frank statements during the debate: '*What amazes me is the ignorance of the Council members regarding the security situation for the past ten years. We need to build real institutions, and we must stop as much as we can the influence of the security forces in politics. We are trying to destroy the power centres in the security forces, but this needs time.*' (Internal Notes PICCR; see also Ibrahim Hamami, *Hidden Hands behind Civil Instability*, 21 June 2005).
22 Hamami, *Hidden Hands*.
23 Amended Basic Law (2003), Article 102 (1).
24 Internal Notes PICCR. Exact statistics on the number of cases lodged against the PNA security organisations before the High Court are not available.
25 Interview with Musa Abu Dhaim, Head of Complaints Section, Palestinian Independent Commission for Citizens' Rights (PICCR), 20 September 2005, Ramallah.
26 Palestinian Independent Commission for Citizens' Rights (PICCR), *Status of the Palestinian Citizens' Rights*, pp. 61-89. Interview with Maen Ida'is, Head of Research, Palestinian Independent Commission for Citizens' Rights (PICCR), 15 September 2005, Ramallah; Interview Musa Abu Dhaim. Proper statistics on non-implemented court decisions are not available.
27 The PICCR, the Centre for Democracy and Workers' Rights, *Al-Mezan* and the Palestinian Center for Human Rights have also represented civilians before the courts in cases of unlawful detention and other violations.

28   *Article 59* of the *Palestinian Elections Law No. 13 of 1995* states that '*it is the responsibility of the security forces to uphold public order and protect the security of the citizens during all phases of the elections.*' The same article also bans any individuals except for security personnel from carrying arms in events related to elections.

29   *Amended Basic Law (2003), Article 30 (1)* states that '*submitting a case to court is a protected and guaranteed right for all people. Each Palestinian shall have the right to seek redress in the judicial system.*'

30   *Article 31* of the *Amended Basic Law (2003)*: '*An independent commission for human rights shall be established pursuant to a law that will specify its formation, duties and jurisdiction. The commission shall submit its reports to the President of the National Authority and to the Palestinian Legislative Council.*'

31   In 2004, for example, no deaths in custody and only one 'disappearance' (detention of individuals in unofficial detention centres belonging to the security organisations) were recorded. Also, cases of politically motivated arrests and torture dropped significantly. Palestinian Independent Commission for Citizens' Rights (PICCR), *Status of the Palestinian Citizens' Rights*, pp. 143-155.

Security Sector Reform and Judicial Reform: The Missing Link

Maen Id'ais

Security sector reform (SSR) in the Palestinian National Authority (PNA) is closely related to Palestinian judicial reform. Both sector reforms aim to establish and develop the rule of law, which includes fighting crime, enforcing the law in the streets and providing security for the Palestinian citizenry. Judicial reform in the PNA is of specific importance as the Judiciary has long been the weakest branch of the Authority.

Protecting law and order and prosecuting lawbreakers generally constitute an integrated cycle. According to Palestinian law, the PNA security organisations are the primary instrument for the Authority to uphold law and order; the Judiciary takes the necessary penal measures against criminals. The functional responsibilities of the security agencies and the Judiciary and their effectiveness in fulfilling them are dependent upon each other: if the security organisations fail to implement the law in the streets, it will be difficult for the Judiciary to hold lawbreakers accountable in the courts. Conversely, if the Judiciary fails in terms of prosecution, even the most effective security agencies will have limited impact. Therefore, reforms on the level of the PNA security organisations should ideally be accompanied by parallel reforms in the Judiciary. Separating SSR and judicial reform or favouring one reform track at the expense of the other are unlikely to yield sustainable progress. This chapter deals with the relation between SSR and judicial reforms. It describes reform efforts in the Palestinian justice system and examines the practical cooperation between the Judiciary and the various security branches. Based on this analysis, the chapter spells out recommendations on how reforms in both sectors could be pushed ahead.

Judicial Reform in the PNA

Past Reform Efforts

Reforming the Judiciary and strengthening the rule of law in the PNA-administered areas was declared a priority by various governments in past years. Since 2001 the PNA has undertaken several reform steps to improve the Palestinian justice system.[1]

Judicial Legislation: Between 2001 and 2003, the PNA issued a package of laws addressing various aspects of judicial reform. These laws included

- the *Basic Law of 2002* and its amendments in 2003 and 2005;
- the *Law of the Judicial Authority No. 1 of 2002*;
- the *Law of the Formation of Regular Courts No. 5 of 2001*;
- the *Penal Procedure Law No. 3 of 2001*;
- the *Law of Civil and Commercial Procedure No. 2 of 2001*;
- the *Law of Evidence in Civil and Commercial Articles No. 4 of 2001*.

Through their enactment the PNA made significant steps towards consolidating the legal status of the Judiciary.

Court of Cassation: The *Law of the Formation of Regular Courts No. 5 of 2001*, enacted by the then President Yasser Arafat in 2001, provided for a Court of Cassation with the authority to review all civil and penal cases dealt with by lower courts. The Court of Appeal officially started its work in 2003.

Increase in Judicial Staff: Over the past three years, the number of judges in Palestinian courts was raised significantly, especially at the first instance. In 2002, more than 30 judges were appointed in Magistrate Courts; in 2003, 19 new Magistrate judges, some of them with prior experience in public prosecution, were appointed; in 2005, eight Magistrate judges were appointed. Additionally, a number of judges were promoted from Magistrate Courts to Courts of First Instance, or from Courts of First Instance to the High Court. Most of the current prosecutors in the Public Prosecution were appointed in 2003. However, appointments did not always rely on clear rules and procedures.

Judicial Infrastructure: An integrated building containing the Court of Cassation and the High Judicial Council – the highest administrative decision-making body in judicial affairs – was constructed in the West Bank city of Ramallah. Further buildings were erected for the Court of First Instance in Bethlehem and a number of Magistrate Courts in the West Bank, including Dura and Halhul in the Hebron Governorate, and Gaza.

Financial Situation of Judicial Staff: The PNA improved the financial status of judges and public prosecutors through the *Law of the Judicial Authority No. 1 of 2002* which regulated salaries and allowances for judicial personnel and increased their salaries.

Abolition of State Security Courts: As part of the PNA's efforts to streamline the court system and remove parallel judicial mechanisms, the Ministry of Justice in 2003 abolished the State Security Courts. These courts had been created by President Arafat in 1995 and had the specific task of trying Palestinian militants engaging in operations against Israel. The ministerial decisions transferred all cases dealt with by the State Security Courts to regular courts.

Expansion of Jurisdiction of Magistrate Courts: With the enactment of the *Law of the Formation of Regular Courts No. 5 of 2001* the jurisdictional amount of the Magistrates Courts – the value of claims the courts were authorised to adjudicate over – was increased from 250 Jordanian Dinars (JD) to 20,000 JD; later it was reduced to 10,000 JD.[2] Consequently, a large number of cases suddenly fell within the jurisdiction of the Magistrate Courts. This step was intended to ease the workload of higher courts. However, it soon turned out that the expansion of jurisdiction was not commensurate with the increase of staff in the Magistrate Courts.

The Need for Further Reforms

Notwithstanding the progress that was made in various areas, the PNA Judiciary as a whole has remained weak and ineffective. Some reform measures had little practical effect although well-intended, others were meant to deflect from the more serious problems in the justice system such as factionalism, corruption and political manipulation. The political will to establish an effective and truly independent Judiciary was clearly missing for many years. Attempts by the government to reinvigorate judicial reform, such as in the context of the Palestinian Comprehensive Reform Programme of 2004 and 2005, had no impact. The Judiciary continues to be plagued by serious shortcomings, with the result that the justice system has failed to put an end to the security chaos on the Palestinian streets.

Role of the Attorney-General: *Article 107 Amended Basic Law (2003)* stipulates that the Attorney-General be approved by the Palestinian Legislative Council (PLC) after his/her appointment by the PNA President. Since the inception of the PNA in 1994 a number of Attorney-Generals were appointed. However, none of the appointed Attorney-Generals has ever received parliamentary approval. The President selected and appointed individuals for the post on the basis of political loyalty rather than professional qualification. Against this background, it is no wonder that there has been very little willingness on the part of the Attorney-General to take decisive measures to enhance the rule of law.

Conflicts between Judicial Stakeholders: Conflicts of jurisdiction and power struggles between various judicial institutions persist, chiefly between the Ministry of Justice and the High Judicial Council. This conflict is over the administrative supervision of courts and public prosecution; it is exacerbated by personal rivalries and continues to paralyse the judicial reform process. Although the government issued a numbers of decrees to regulate the matter, a solution has yet to be found. The amended *Law of the Judicial Authority No. 15 of 2005*, drafted in the frame of the Palestinian Comprehensive Reform

Programme, set out to redefine the authorities of both institutions. However, the law was rejected in November 2005 by the PNA High Court in its capacity of Constitutional Court, due to violations of the legislative process.

Weakness of the Military Judiciary: Many violations of the law are committed by members of the security organisations.[3] However, the PNA Military Judiciary has never been able to live up to its responsibility of holding security personnel accountable. As the table below indicates, the numbers of cases dealt with by the Military Judiciary has seen a sharp drop over the last few years. Structurally the Military Judiciary suffers from unclear authorities and ineffective organisation, and there is no PNA legislation regulating its work.

Table 1: Number of Cases Heard by Military Judiciary

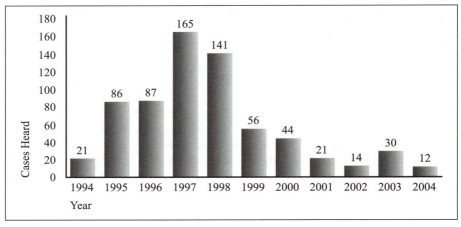

Lack of Comprehensive Legal Framework: There are currently no laws for the PNA Constitutional Court and the Administrative Courts which would regulate their structure, jurisdiction and procedures. Despite a proclamation by the government that the drafting of pertinent legislation would be pushed ahead, very little progress has been made in practice.

Dysfunctionality of the Courts of First Instance: The *Law of the Formation of Regular Courts No. 5 of 2001* provided for the formation of panels with three judges at the Courts of First Instance. However, although the number of cases pending with these courts dropped after the increase in the jurisdictional amount of Magistrate Courts, the newly-introduced panels remained unable to deal with the cases presented to them. Judges were not attending court sessions on a regular basis, and the overall number of judges at the Courts of First Instance remained relatively low. The PNA tried to remedy these problems by amendments in the law which under specific circumstances allow individual judges to handle cases at the Courts of First Instance[4]; however, this measure has done practically nothing to ameliorate the situation.

Lack of Judicial Inspection: Judicial inspection is still inefficient; no palpable steps have been taken to tackle the lack of administrative oversight over the courts. In fact, judicial inspection is a major bone of contention between the Ministry of Justice and the High Judicial Council and resulted in conflicts between the Minister and the Steering Committee for the Development of the Judiciary which coordinates the judicial reform process. The Ministry repeatedly refused to give the High Judicial Council the authority for inspection, arguing[5] that it would be unacceptable to grant the Judiciary the right to oversee itself.

Case Backlog: The accumulation of cases in the courts has long been a major problem. The situation, however, has deteriorated during the past two years through the expansion of the jurisdictional amount of the Magistrate Courts which caused a massive increase in cases for the lower instance. Another aggravating factor is the low compliance of witnesses with summonses, leading to long procedural delays. Often witnesses refuse to testify in court unless the defence pays them money or provides them with free transportation.

Qualification and Training: The recruitment of additional judges for the Magistrate Courts has not been sufficient, if compared with the actual needs of a functional judicial system. There is still a lack of qualified judges and judicial training institutions in Palestine. The PLC has not yet finalised the drafting of the *Law Concerning the Judicial Training Institute*. Clear regulations relating to the transfer and promotion of judges and public prosecution officers are missing.

The Relations between the Judiciary and the Security Branches

The Legal Framework

All PNA security personnel enjoy certain powers in order to maintain public order and security. However, it is the prerogative of the Public Prosecution to authorise the investigation of crimes and the arrest of suspects. In terms of execution, this function lies with the *Criminal Investigations Department* of the *Civil Police* which acts as the so-called 'Judicial Police.' In fact, the *Civil Police* is the only security organisation which has the official legal authority to conduct searches and arrests in all criminal cases.[6] The *Penal Procedure Law No. 3 of 2001* specifies the powers of the *Police* in fighting crime and spells out who is included under 'Judicial Police.' Nevertheless, other PNA security agencies, including *Preventive Security* and *Military Intelligence*, illegally detain and interrogate citizens.

Article 21 Penal Procedure Law No. 3 of 2001 defines the officials who enjoy the authority of the 'Judicial Police' as follows:

- The Chief of Police and his deputies;
- Police Commanders at the Governorate and District level;
- Police officers and non-commissioned officers in their area of responsibility (Criminal Investigation Department);
- Commanders of naval vessels and aerial vehicles;
- Officials who are statutorily invested with judicial powers outside the Police.

The *Law of the Judicial Authority No. 1 of 2002* and the *Penal Procedure Law No. 3 of 2001* link the 'Judicial Police' to the Public Prosecution. The *Law of the Judicial Authority No. 1 of 2002* states in *Article 69* that '*members of the Judicial Police shall be, with regard to their functions, affiliated to the Public Prosecution.*' The *Penal Procedure Law No. 3 of 2001* states in *Article 19 (1)* that '*members of the Public Prosecution shall assume the duties of Judicial Police and oversee judicial officers, each within his own sphere of competence.*' In terms of accountability, *Article 20* of the law grants oversight authority to the Attorney-General:

> 'The Attorney-General shall supervise the judicial police officers and they shall be subject to his oversight in regard of the acts of their function; the Attorney-General shall be

entitled to request competent authorities to take disciplinary measures against each person violating his obligations or failing in his function.'

Article 19 (2) of the *Penal Procedure Law No. 3 of 2001* gives 'Judicial Police' personnel the authority to '*conduct searches and investigations of crimes and their perpetrators and collect evidence which is necessary for investigation of the action.*' *Article 22* enumerates the powers of 'Judicial Police' as:

- Receiving complaints and reports about crimes and transferring them to the Public Prosecution;
- Conducting examinations and searches and obtaining clarifications necessary to facilitate the investigation;
- Questioning experts and witnesses not under oath;
- Taking all measures necessary to preserve evidence of crime;
- Writing the official minutes relating to all procedures.

The *Penal Procedure Law No. 3 of 2001* contains rather detailed provisions in relation to the duties of the *Police*. According to *Article 27*, 'Judicial Police' personnel '*must proceed immediately to the scene of the crime in order to inspect and secure the material evidence*' in the case of felonies or misdemeanours.[7] *Police* personnel must further '*establish the condition of the premises, of persons and of everything which may serve to make the truth manifest, and hear the testimony of whoever is present at the scene or of any person capable of furnishing information on the crime and its perpetrators.*' The *Police* are required to immediately notify the Public Prosecution which must attend the scene of crime in cases of flagrant felony. Procedures of arrest are stated in detail in *Article 30*. 'Judicial Police' personnel may arrest without notice any individual under the following categories:

- Individuals caught in the act of committing crimes or misdemeanours which require imprisonment for more than six months;
- Individuals resisting the Police while fleeing or attempting to flee from places of detention if they were detained in a legal manner;
- Individuals committing or being accused of committing a crime and refusing to give their name and address to the Police or lacking a known or permanent residence in Palestine.

In all other cases, the 'Judicial Police' must request the Public Prosecution to issue an arrest warrant in accordance with *Article 31*.

Article 38 Penal Procedure Law No. 3 of 2001 regulates the searching of individuals. 'Judicial Police' personnel may undertake body searches only in the case of lawful arrest. In this event, the *Police* must draw up a list of seized possessions, sign it together with the arrested individual and hand a copy to the arrested person. Entering and searching houses and other premises is only allowed on the basis of a search warrant issued by the Public Prosecution in accordance with *Article 39*. *Article 49* allows 'Judicial Police' officers to seek assistance from other police or military forces in performing their duties.

The conduct of criminal investigation is the exclusive prerogative of the Public[8] Prosecution, as stated in *Article 55 (1)* of the *Penal Procedure Law No. 3 of 2001*. As shown above, however, certain investigative powers may be delegated to the *Police*. *Article 55 (2)* gives the Attorney-General or the respective prosecutor the right '*to authorise one of the officers of the competent judicial officer corps to perform any of the acts of investigation in a specific case, except for the interrogation of the accused in a felony.*' Such authorisation must be specific and not amount to a general waiver.[9]

Cooperation between Public Prosecution and Civil Police

There are various factors impairing the work of the *Civil Police* in their capacity as 'Judicial Police.' These problems primarily affect the *Criminal Investigations Departments* and relate to both its capacity and its relations with the Public Prosecution. The result are serious shortcomings in the investigation of crimes and the prosecution of suspects.[10]

Ineffective Collaboration: Collaboration between the *Police* and the Public Prosecution is ineffective. This is partly due to the lack of proper training and knowledge of procedures, partly due to conflicts of interest interfering with the work of the *Police*. For example, in several governorates *Criminal Investigations Departments* customarily notify the Public Prosecution of crimes against 'unidentified individuals' but also fail to identify the perpetrator of these crimes. Such dysfunctional processing of information by the *Police* prevents any effective action by the Public Prosecution. In other areas, the Public Prosecution does not admit cases in which it deems, often wrongly, that the *Police* conducted incomplete investigations. Both practices are very detrimental to the effective persecution of crime.

Poor Knowledge of the Law among the Police: *Police* officers acting in the capacity of 'Judicial Police' lack knowledge and understanding of the powers and duties assigned to them. A good example is the widespread confusion among the *Police* concerning the modalities of transferring detainees to the Public Prosecution. *Article 34* of the *Penal Procedure Law No. 3 of 2001* states as follows in this regard:

> 'The judicial officer is obliged to hear the statement of the person arrested immediately and, if such person fails to come forward with justification for his release, to send him within 24 hours to the competent deputy prosecutor.'

However, as 'Judicial Police' officers sometimes found the 24 hours period insufficient for questioning suspects, different interpretations of the law have evolved. According to one view, the period stated in the law is adequate for a preliminary investigation after which the suspect is either released or transferred to the Public Prosecution for further investigation. This interpretation is in line with the law, which gives the Public Prosecution the main responsibility for investigating crimes.

According to a second view, the 24 hours period is impracticable because it does not allow the Police to gather sufficient evidence for transferring a suspect to the Prosecution. This interpretation reflects the fact that the Public Prosecution often rejects a case if the Police does not provide sufficient information for convicting a suspect.

Thus, Police officers sometimes feel that their duty to gather sufficient evidence, as stated in *Article 19 (1)* of the *Penal Procedure Law No. 3 of 2001*[11], overrides the 24 hours period stated in *Article 34*.

Faulty Delegation of Investigative Powers to the Police: Delegating investigative powers from the Public Prosecution to the *Police*, as provided for in *Article 55 (2)* of the *Penal Procedure Law No. 3 of 2001* encounters various practical and legal problems:

■ *Verbal Authorisation*: The *Police* often do not receive written authorisation to carry out criminal investigations. Rather, the Public Prosecution issues an investigative order over the telephone and provides a written authorisation only after having received the complete case from the *Police*. Verbal authorisations regularly fail to determine the scope, duration and conditions of an investigation. This amounts to a carte blanche for the 'Judicial Police' regarding the methods of investigation. The resulting violations of the law not only infringe upon the rights of citizens but also impair adjudication, as courts might have to release suspects due to procedural errors. Furthermore, verbal authorisation makes effective oversight on the part of the Prosecution almost impossible.

■ *General Authorisation*: *Article 55 (3)* of the *Penal Procedure Law No. 3 of 2001* explicitly bans general authorisations. In reality, however, general authorisations are the norm. In many cases the Prosecution does not mandate specific 'Judicial Police' officers with an investigation but issues a general order to investigate the crime as a whole. This practice has contributed to the Prosecution's habit of not accepting incomplete investigation files from the *Police*.

■ *Interrogation*: The *Penal Procedure Law No. 3 of 2001* in *Article 55 (2)* explicitly bans the 'Judicial Police' from interrogating suspects of felonies on behalf of the Prosecution. However, in reality the *Police* often does hold interrogations in felony cases, although they are commonly not taken under oath as the *Police* anticipates their rejection by the courts. This practice is a grave violation of citizens' rights, especially because such interrogation notes are often used by the Prosecution to charge suspects.

■ *Weak Oversight of the 'Judicial Police'*: Although technically affiliated to the Prosecution, the 'Judicial Police' is not subject to effective judicial oversight. In practice the Prosecution has failed to establish the institutional supremacy it is given by the law. Indeed, the *Police* generally sees itself as more capable of investigating crimes than the Prosecution and regularly exceeds its mandate on the basis of unlawful general authorisations. The Prosecution lacks the institutional weight and necessary tools to redress these violations.

■ *Interference of PNA Security Branches with the Police*: Other PNA security organisations such as the *Preventive Security* or the *Military Intelligence* regularly interfere with the work of the *Police*. These agencies do not fall under 'Judicial Police' as defined in *Article 21* of the *Penal Procedure Law No. 3 of 2001* but arrest, interrogate and prosecute suspects in the absence of any legal basis. As the courts do not recognise evidence and confessions obtained – often under torture – by these agencies, many criminals have escaped punishment on the grounds of procedural errors.

Collaboration between Public Prosecution and other PNA Security Organisations

Although collaboration between the Judiciary and the *Police* is flawed, there is at least a legal framework in place that aims to regulate the relations between these institutions. This is not the case with regard to other PNA security organisations, especially agencies with intelligence functions such as the *Preventive Security* and the *Military Intelligence*. In fact, relations between the Judiciary and these agencies are highly problematic. The *General Intelligence* is something of an exception in that it was legally entitled to act as 'Judicial Police' through the *General Intelligence Law No. 12 of 2005*. However, for many years, the *General Intelligence* has been equally involved in illegal detentions, and it remains to be seen if the new legal provision changes much in practice.

Non-Implementation of Court Decisions: Ever since 1994, the security organisations have systematically refused to implement court decisions. This has been especially grave in the case of High Court decisions to release unlawfully detained prisoners. Although the number of such decisions has dropped over the past few years – mainly due to the destruction of the Palestinian security infrastructure which by default resulted in fewer arrests –, the security agencies still fail to implement court orders, especially in property and financial disputes. This is partly a consequence of the Israeli ban on PNA security branches accessing Areas B and C where Israel has jurisdiction over security under the *Oslo II Agreement*; however, with respect to Area A – where the PNA has explicit jurisdiction over security – the responsibility for the poor implementation of court orders lies solely with the PNA itself.

Unlawful Detentions: As outlined above, the *Preventive Security*, the *Military Intelligence* and until recently the *General Intelligence* have been systematically detaining and interrogating suspects in contravention of the *Penal Procedure Law No. 3 of 2001*. This refers primarily but not exclusively to collaborators with the Israeli occupation, especially those who assisted in the assassination of Palestinian resistance activists. In this context, all PNA intelligence agencies set up their own detention centres which are separated from the official PNA prisons. The *Law Concerning Correction and Rehabilitation Centres No. 6 of 1998* does not apply in these installations, and suspects have been held for years without any procedural safeguards or judicial supervision. Also, the minimum detention conditions set forth in the law are commonly not met in these centres.

Torture and Death in Custody: Detainees in illegal detention centres are often subject to torture, in clear contravention of the *Amended Basic Law (2003)*, the *Penal Procedure Law No. 3 of 2001* and the 'Al-Khadr'Decision of the Ramallah Court of First Instance of 1998.[12] In many cases, PNA security branches submit evidence obtained under torture to the courts. Furthermore, some 30 citizens have died in detention centres belonging to PNA intelligence branches over the past ten years. No judicial investigation took place in these cases.

Creeping Assumption of Vetting Authority: PNA intelligence organisations have replaced the Judiciary in giving good conduct and non-conviction certificates to people who wish to take up a public office. According to the procedures of the PNA General Personnel Council, an 'Institutions Security Department' which is affiliated to the *Preventive Security* ensures that applicants for a public position have security clearance. The department can also request that the General Personnel Council sack employees on grounds of security. In the absence of judicial supervision, political or personal interference in the process is the norm.[13]

Insufficient Protection of the Judicial Personnel and Infrastructure: The PNA security organisations are responsible for the protection of judicial installations and personnel. However, the security agencies have failed to deliver adequate protection, with courts, judges and lawyers being attacked on a regular basis. Although the Palestinian Bar Association has staged several protests in this regard, the Executive has not taken decisive measures to defend the Judiciary against assaults.[14] The lack of physical protection also affects the PNA Correction and Rehabilitation Centres under the control of the Civil Police[15.]

Conclusion

The dysfunctionality of the PNA Judiciary has been discussed in dozens of studies, workshops and seminars. The deficiencies of the Palestinian justice system and the factors militating against reform have been meticulously analysed; in fact, the diagnosis is obvious, and the problem does not require further scrutiny. Yet, despite various attempts, no real progress towards a strong and effective Judiciary has been made. On the contrary, it seems that the capacities of the Palestinian justice system have further deteriorated. Tens of thousands of cases are pending in the courts and the implementation gap in relation to court decisions persists. As a result, traditional mechanisms of dispute resolution have gained prominence; according to a 2005 poll, only 26 per cent of the Palestinians have a high level of trust in the PNA justice system, as opposed to 37 per cent who place high trust in the Palestinian clan-based customary law.[16] Moreover, no effective measures have been taken to bridge the institutional gap between the security branches and the Judiciary, or to coordinate what little has been achieved in judicial reform with the ongoing SSR process.

Indeed, the Judiciary continues to be marginalised by the PNA, specifically the Executive, despite repeated public commitments to reform. The main reason behind this marginalisation is that the PNA has no interest in a strong justice system, for fear that it will prosecute those in the Executive who are responsible for administrative and financial corruption.

It shall be emphasised here that the responsibility for the current lawlessness in the PNA-controlled areas lies primarily with the Authority itself. It is true that Israeli occupation has had a negative impact on the PNA's capacity to enforce law and order. However, it is not true that the increasing number of violations committed by security personnel is an outcome of the occupation and that the Authority is unable to put an end to this. Likewise, it is not correct that the Israeli occupation authorities prevent individuals and officials from being held accountable through the courts. In other words, the PNA can take effective steps to improve the rule of law and the security of the citizens, if only the political will is there to do so.

Providing security for the Palestinian citizenry requires functioning law-enforcement mechanisms and effective cooperation between the *Police* and the Judiciary in particular. To this effect, a number of steps should be taken in the security branches and the Judiciary. In order to secure the sustainability of reform, SSR and judicial reform measures should be implemented in parallel. A steering committee with strong political backing should coordinate the process. With respect to the PNA security organisations, the following should be done:

■ Enacting of legislation that governs the work of the *Civil Police* and clearly regulates the remits, responsibilities and powers of the police service, as well as its relationship to other security agencies.
■ Restricting the role of the 'Judicial Police' to its remits as laid out in the *Penal Procedure Law No. 3 of 2001* and amending the law where necessary to clarify the relations between the *Police* and the Public Prosecution. This is especially important in order to prevent situations where criminal suspects escape punishment due to procedural errors during investigation.
■ Completing of procedures to set forth legislation that regulates the work of other PNA security branches, in particular *Preventive Security* and *Military Intelligence*, and making sure this legislation is commensurate with civil-democratic standards.
■ Drafting and implementing of a security plan in order to guarantee adequate protection of judicial institutions and personnel including court buildings, Public Prosecution officials and judges. A serious investigation into past security violations, public announcement of the results and prosecution of perpetrators would be an important symbol here.
■ Setting forth of procedures and plans to ensure that correction and rehabilitation centres are duly protected against attacks. In relation to the Judiciary, the following steps are necessary:
■ Devising and implementing of a sound reform strategy for the Judiciary with achievable and realistic objectives. Such a strategy should take into account progress on the security reform track and be synchronised with it, especially in the area of law-enforcement.
■ Creating of an environment conducive to reform through forcing the retirement of judicial officials who block reform.
■ Strengthening of the Public Prosecution in order to give it back its original responsibility for investigating crimes and prosecuting criminals. This means primarily restricting the 'Judicial Police' to the auxiliary role it is given by the law.
■ Finalising and where necessary amending of all legislation relating to the Judiciary, such as the *Judicial Authority Draft Law of 2005*.
■ Improving of human, material and financial resources of the courts so that they can deal with the case backlog. This has to include a thorough reorganisation of the

Courts of First Instance, as well as the hiring and training of new judicial personnel.

- Devising and implementing of an integrated and effective system of judicial inspection, based on a clear division of responsibilities between the Ministry of Justice and the High Judicial Council.
- Reorganising of the Military Judiciary and strengtheningof the capacities of Military Courts to enable them to effectively hold accountable security personnel responsible for violations of the law. This includes enacting a sound legal framework regulating the functions and responsibilities of the Military Courts.

Notes

1   The PNA Judiciary is divided into Magistrate Courts, Courts of First Instance and a High Court; the High Court simultaneously functions as the Constitutional Court, the Administrative Court and the Court of Appeal. The regular courts deal with all types of crimes and civil claims, administrative issues are only dealt with by the High Court.
2   *Law No. 2 Concerning the Amendment of Some of the Provisions of the Law of the Formation of Regular Courts No. 5 of 2001.*
3   Director of the Military Judiciary Body, *Al Hayat Al-Jadidah,* 27 February 2005.
4   *Law No. 2 of 2005 Amending the Law of the Formation of Regular Courts No. 5 of 2001.*
5   Statement by the Minister of Justice at a workshop held by the Centre for the Development of the Private Sector on the 'National Committee on Reform and its Performance', 29 December 2005.
6   Since the enactment of the *General Intelligence Law No. 17 of 2005,* the *General Intelligence* also has the authority to act as 'Judicial Police', but only within its remits *(Article 12: 'The Intelligence in the cause of the commencement of its jurisdiction set forth under this Law shall have the capacity of the judicial police.')* This is a new provision not yet put to the test.
7   In terms of gravity, the law divides crimes into contraventions, misdemeanours and felonies. Contraventions are penalised with a fine or confinement for a period not more than one week. Misdemeanours are crimes penalised with imprisonment between one week and three years. Felonies are crimes penalised with more than three years of imprisonment. *Jordanian Penal Law No. 16 of 1969, Article 14-16.*
8   *Article 1* of the *Penal Procedure Law No. 3 of 2001* states that *'the right to file and conduct a penal action is vested exclusively in the Public Prosecution, and it shall not be filed by others except in those cases where the law provides otherwise.'* [9] Ibid., *Article 55 (3): 'The authorisation may not be general.'*
10 The following remarks are based on the findings of two PICCR workshops, one with the leadership of the *Criminal Investigations Department* in Ramallah on 18 August 2004 and one with police officers and experts in Jericho on 25 and 26 August 2005 ('The Judiciary and Security'). The recommendations of the latter were officially approved by the Council of Ministers.
11 *Penal Procedure Law No. 3 of 2001, Article 19: 'The members of the Public Prosecution shall* exercise judicial powers and supervise officers invested with judicial powers each within the *circuit of his jurisdiction.'*
12 On 23 March 1998, the Court of First Instance in Ramallah acquitted nine individuals charged with murder on the grounds of procedural errors. The Court decided that the confessions of the suspects, who had been detained by the *Military Intelligence,* had been extracted under torture and were therefore null and void. Furthermore, the Court ruled that the cooperation between *Military Intelligence* and Public Prosecution in the case was unlawful.

13 See PICCR, *Report on the Role of Security Agencies in the Public Function*, Ramallah 2004.

14 On 14 June 2005, the Council of Ministers established a special committee to discuss attacks on courts, judges, members of the public prosecution and court staff. The Committee – composed of the Ministers of the Interior and National Security, Justice, and Finance – was tasked to devise a security plan for the Judiciary; however, the Committee in fact did not deliver anything.

15 In late 2004 and early 2005, two serious incidents resulted in the killing of five detainees in *Civil Police* Correction and Rehabilitation Centres. On 1 October 2004, a group of armed individuals wearing Israeli military uniforms raided the prison in the city of Nablus, handcuffed the police officers guarding the prison and released two prisoners. The assailants also killed one prisoner inside the prison and another one at the gate. On 10 February 2005, dozens of armed individuals raided the central prison in Gaza city and killed three detainees. In both incidents, the police forces could not protect the centres and detainees therein.

16 Bocco, R., De Martino, L., Luethold, A., Friedrich, R., *Palestinian Public Perceptions of Security Sector Governance, Summary Report*, DCAF/IUED, Geneva, 21 November 2005, p. 9.

Non-Statutory Armed Groups and Security Sector Governance

Mohammad Najib and Roland Friedrich

Since the creation of the Palestinian National Authority (PNA) in 1994, Palestinian security sector governance has been characterised by the parallel existence of statutory and non-statutory security actors.[1] One might argue that the differentiation between statutory and non-statutory armed groups is faulty in the Palestinian context anyway, given that the PNA does not constitute a sovereign state but merely a transitory political regime based on an agreement between a state and a non-state organisation. Nevertheless, it is possible to distinguish between security actors who operate inside the framework of the *Oslo Agreements* and who have an official mandate to use force and others who operate outside this framework. The PNA security organisations form the first category. To the latter belong various armed groups.

In practice, however, it is difficult to draw clear lines of distinction between statutory and non-statutory actors, as there are many overlaps in terms of operational activities, membership affiliation and ideology. The lines have become even more blurred since the outbreak of the second *Intifada* in 2000, in the course of which non-statutory armed groups gained considerable influence and political weight. In many ways, the rise of these groups was a direct result of the almost complete destruction of Palestinian security infrastructure by the Israeli army in 2001 and 2002.

This chapter is divided in two parts. The first section offers a description of the major politically relevant armed groups in the Palestinian arena, namely the armed wings of Hamas, Islamic Jihad and the Popular Resistance Committees (PRCs), as well as the *Al-Aqsa Martyrs Brigades*.[2] This section also looks at the ideology, strategy and operational capacities of these groups. The second section examines the challenge that non-statutory security actors pose to Palestinian security sector governance. It also explores options for the Palestinian security sector to deal with it. This issue has attracted special relevance since Hamas took over government after the January 2006 parliamentary elections.

An Overview of Palestinian Non-Statutory Armed Groups

Izz ad-Din al-Qassam Brigades

The *Izz ad-Din al-Qassam Brigades* are the military wing of Hamas *(Harakat al-Muqawama al-Islamiya)*, the Islamic Resistance Movement. According to Hamas, the *Izz ad-Din al-Qassam Brigades* were formally established in summer 1991 when Hamas operatives assassinated the Rabbi of Kfar Darom, a former settlement in Gaza; the first armed units were set up by Zakaria Waleed Aqel. Thus, the official announcement of Hamas' military wing came nearly four years after the establishment of the movement itself, which took place in December 1987, shortly after the outbreak of the first *Inti-*

fada. The *Izz ad-Din al-Qassam Brigades* were mainly composed of younger Hamas activists who had gone underground during the Israeli arrest campaign of 1990, which followed the so-called 'war of the knives.'[3]

However, various individuals who later attained senior positions in *Izz ad-Din al-Qassam* had been involved in armed activities prior to the *Intifada*. From 1984 on, senior Islamists in Gaza such as Sheikh Ahmad Yassin and Sheikh Salah Shehada had been making efforts to develop an armed capacity to resist the Israeli occupation. In 1986, Sheikh Shehada[4], following orders from Sheikh Yassin, established a network of Islamic militants named *Al-Mujahidoun al-Filastinioun* ('Palestinian Fighters'); yet the Israeli authorities arrested most members of the group and confiscated its weaponry. At the same time, Sheikh Yassin gave order to establish the *Majd*, a security branch that was in charge of hunting down collaborators. In the West Bank, cells affiliated with the Muslim Brotherhood had been operating under the name of the *Abdallah Azzam Brigades*.

Ideology

As the military wing of Hamas, the *Izz ad-Din al-Qassam Brigades* operate under the ideological and doctrinal guidance of the movement. Hamas is an outgrowth of the Muslim Brotherhood and shares many of its reform-oriented Islamist tenets, such as the view that Islam constitutes a belief system which regulates all aspects of life ('Islam is the solution') and that preaching, education, and charitable activities promote Islamic faith.[5]

However, the Israeli-Palestinian conflict and its dynamics have also much shaped Hamas. Armed struggle against Israel came to constitute a core element in the thinking of the Palestinian branch of the Muslim Brotherhood, especially its Gaza wing. Since its inception in 1987, Hamas' view of the conflict has been oscillating between a religious-doctrinal perspective, in which the struggle with Israel is seen as a conflict between Islam and Judaism, and a political perspective, in which the struggle is about resistance to foreign occupation, Zionism and Western imperialism, all of which are seen as closely interlinked.

The first perspective dominated Hamas' thinking during its first four years. The second gained prominence with the political and organisational maturing of the movement.[6] A good example of the first perspective is the Hamas Charter of 1987. In this text, the religious discourse prevails and Palestine is defined as an '*Islamic land entrusted to Muslim generations until Judgement Day*';[7] Hamas' 'Introductory Memorandum', approved in the mid-1990s, emphasises a more political and pragmatic perspective where the notion of liberating the land and ending the occupation is of greater importance than Islamist tenets. According to the 'Introductory Memorandum', the struggle is with the

> 'Zionist enemy who is associated with the Western Project to bring the Arab Islamic umma under the domination of Western culture, to make it dependent on the West, and to perpetuate its underdevelopment.'[8]

The Palestinian people are '*the direct target of the Zionist settler occupation*' and '*must bear the main burden of resisting the unjust occupation.*'[9] Hamas views the struggle as a long-term and historic one: '*There must be incessant resistance to and confrontation with the enemy in Palestine until we achieve victory and liberation.*'[10] To this effect, Hamas relies on the support of the Arab-Islamic nation *(umma)*: '*The Arab and Islamic countries are regions from which our Palestinian people can draw support.*'[11]

However, a variety of internal and external factors, such as the establishment of the Palestinian National Authority in 1994 and pressure from the international community have propelled Hamas to develop a high degree of flexibility. The movement has constantly tried to strike a balance between what it terms the 'historical solution' – the liberation of all Palestine which is an '*indivisible unit, from its north to its south (...), its sea to its river*'[12] – and the interim solution, a Palestinian state in the West Bank and Gaza Strip on the pre-1967 borders. The 'Change and Reform Platform' approved by Hamas in the run-up to the 2006 parliamentary elections[13] and the so-called 'Prisoners' Document' of June 2006 are written expressions of the interim solution.[14] Hamas also became keen not to antagonise state actors inside and outside the region and to avoid political isolation. Finally, Hamas increasingly underlined the importance of popular participation in politics and developed its own vision of democracy; this process culminated in its participation in the January 2006 Palestinian parliamentary elections and the subsequent formation of a Hamasled PNA government.

Mission and Strategy

The *Izz ad-Din al-Qassam Brigades* aim at liberating Palestine through military action. They see themselves in a tradition of Palestinian resistance dating back to the British mandate period.[15] Officially, *Izz ad-Din al-Qassam* have the following mission:

> 'To contribute in the effort of liberating Palestine and restoring the rights of the Palestinian people under the sacred Islamic teachings of the Holy Quran, the Sunna (traditions) of Prophet Mohammad (peace and blessings ofAllah be upon him) and the traditions of Muslim rulers and scholars noted for their piety and dedication.'[16]

This objective translates into three policy priorities:

> 'To evoke the spirit of Jihad (resistance) amongst Palestinians, Arabs and Muslims; to defend Palestinians and their land against the Zionist occupation and its manifestations; to liberate Palestinians and their land that was usurped by the Zionist occupation forces and settlers.'[17]

In line with the doctrine of Hamas, *Izz ad-Din al-Qassam* members conceive armed struggle as an individual religious duty.[18]

Apart from its ideological dimension, military action also serves Hamas as an important source of mass appeal and political mobilisation. The movement has long been making deliberate use of its 'resistance credentials.' Hamas used them for instance during the 2005 local elections and 2006 parliamentary elections, when it claimed that the Israeli 'disengagement' from Gaza was a result of its military operations.

Officially, military actions by the *Izz ad-Din al-Qassam Brigades* are guided by various principles. These call on the military wing of Hamas:

- 'To restrict its engagements and confrontation only to army units and some armed formations that support them.
- To exercise the right of self-defence against the occupation or raids by armed settlers.
- To focus on military or semi-military targets and to avoid other targets, especially civilians.
- To respect the humanity of the other side under conditions of armed engagements and not to engage in mutilation, defacement or excessive killing.
- Not to target Western individuals or interests in the Occupied Territories or outside.
- Not to carry out any operation outside occupied Palestine and to concentrate the efforts inside the Occupied Territories.'[19]

However, in practice *Izz ad-Din al-Qassam* have adopted a military strategy that includes the targeting of civilians. Yet it is important to note that Hamas' military strategy has undergone various changes in response to the dynamics of the conflict. For the first seven years, Hamas attacked only what it defines as 'legitimate military targets', that is Israeli armed forces personnel and installations. Following the 'Hebron massacre' of 1994[20] and then again after the assassination of military leader 'Engineer' Yahya Ayash by Israeli intelligence in 1996, *Izz ad-Din al-Qassam* embarked on a series of suicide bombings against civilians inside Israel; the movement described this as being in line with the principle of reciprocity. Between 1996 and 2001, the group largely refrained from targeting civilians. This was partly due to the PNA's crackdown on Hamas in 1996. In the second *Intifada* (2000-2005), *Izz ad-Din al-Qassam* were responsible for the bulk of Palestinian suicide bombings in Israel. Having joined the armed uprising relatively late, in January 2001, they acted partly in cooperation with other organisations. Since March 2005, Hamas has been committed to a so-called *tahdi'a* ('period of calm') and refrained largely from operations against Israeli civilians.

Relations between Hamas and Fatah have long been strained. Both movements consider themselves the true representatives of the Palestinian national movement. Up to 2006, Hamas took pains to avoid direct confrontation with Fatah. Its Charter asks Hamas to seek to maintain amicable relations with Fatah and all other Palestinian factions. Between 1996 and 1999, the Fatah-dominated PNA launched a major crackdown on the movement. In April 2006, Hamas, then in government, tried to assert its political control over the Palestinian security forces by establishing a Hamas-dominated security organisation under the PNA Ministry of the Interior, the *Executive Force*. This led for the first time to larger violent clashes between Hamas and Fatah militants.

Strength, Equipment and Tactics

The exact number of *Izz ad-Din al-Qassam* operatives is only known to the organisation itself. Estimates range from 10,000 to 17,000 men under arms, with a majority of operatives based in Gaza.[21] *Izz ad-Din al-Qassam* have adopted a set of recruitment criteria. New members need to fulfil '*the moral requirements of piety, integrity, and steadfastness, as well as the physical and educational requirements for the tasks to be assigned to them.*'[22] Recruits undergo a two-years training process.

The *Izz ad-Din al-Qassam Brigades* are equipped with M-16/M-4 and AK-47 assault rifles, imported and self-produced RPG launchers *(Yassin)* and hand-grenades, mortars of various calibres, as well as the home-produced *Al-Qassam* rocket; the latter has a three-kilogram warhead and a range of between six and eight kilometres (the latest model reportedly has a range of 14 km). In terms of tactics, *Izz ad-Din al-Qassam* have been using shootings of Israeli civilians and combatants and Palestinian civilian collaborators, kidnappings, suicide-bombings, and car-bombings. Between 2002 and March 2005, the organisation increasingly shifted its modus operandi toward the use of high-trajectory fire on Israeli targets. Qassam rockets became Hamas' '*new strategic weapon of choice which replaces the use of martyrdom operations.*'[23]

Israeli military operations have significantly degraded the capabilities of *Izz ad-Din al-Qassam* over the past years. Israel also arrested or killed important military and political leaders. Killed military leaders include Sheikh Salah Shehada (2002), Ibrahim Al-Maqadma, the head of the internal security branch (2003), Mahmoud Abu Hannoud (2001) and Ibrahim Hamed (2006). Important assassinated political leaders are Sheikh Ahmad Yassin (2004), Abdelaziz Rantisi (2004), and Ismail Abu Shanab (2003). According to its own sources, *Izz ad-Din al-Qassam* has lost some 800 members killed since the outbreak of the second *Intifada*.[24]

Command and Control

The military wing of Hamas operates secretly: organisation, command and control, recruitment, training and communication are kept confidential. *Izz ad-Din al-Qassam* are organised in a network of cells over Gaza and the West Bank, which are grouped in 'companies' and 'battalions'. Cells comprise four to five members which work semi-independently of each other under the instructions of the higher leadership. In the past, this command system proved partly counterproductive, as the capture of a cell member by Israeli security forces often quickly led to the identification of the rest of the cell.

The leadership is based inside Palestine; important commanders are Mohammad Deif and Ahmad Ja'abri who reside in Gaza. This is in contrast to the political leadership of Hamas which is split between the 'internal' leadership – the Gaza and West Bank leadership committees – and the 'external'leadership in the form of the Political Bureau, which is based in Damascus. Hamas detainees in Israeli prisons constitute the fourth centre of power. Both leaderships nominally share responsibility for decision-making through the Unified Consultative Council.

Since the late 1990s the balance between 'internal'and 'external'leadership has shifted towards the former. The release of Sheikh Yassin from Israeli detention in 1997, the crackdown by the Jordanian government on Hamas activities in the kingdom in 1999, and the electoral victories of the movement in 2005 and 2006 have facilitated this shift. In 2006, splits became visible between *Izz ad-Din al-Qassam* and Hamas' political leadership in the Palestinian Territories, and the military wing again drew closer to the 'external leadership.'

The *Izz ad-Din al-Qassam Brigades* operate under a high degree of discipline and generally obey decisions of the political leadership. During the 53-days *hudna* ('cease-fire') of summer 2003, the organisation did not conduct any operations; likewise, *Izz ad-Din al-Qassam* have stuck to the *tahdi'a*, except for circumstances where the political leadership ordered otherwise.[25] Until the Hamas takeover of the Gaza Strip in June 2007 – reportedly conducted by its military wing without the blessings of the political echelon – militant operations in the absence of a political decision had been relatively rare.[26]

Financing

The *Izz ad-Din al-Qassam Brigades* receive their funding from the Hamas movement inside and outside the Palestinian Territories. There is a strict separation in Hamas between military funds and money used for political, social or other activities. Iran is the main sponsor of Hamas' military wing, as opposed to the political wing, which is primarily funded by non-governmental organisations from Saudi Arabia and other Gulf states. Iran's financial aid to *Izz ad-Din al-Qassam* amounts to some \$3 million per year, according to unofficial sources. Money is directed to the organisation through charity societies or money changers. An important internal source of revenue are Hamas-owned businesses such as taxi firms and import-export companies.

Jerusalem Battalions (Saraya al-Quds)

Saraya al-Quds is the military wing of the Islamic Jihad in Palestine. The Islamic Jihad was formed in 1981 by two Islamists in Gaza – Fathi Shiqaqi from Rafah and Abd al-Aziz Awda from Jabaliya – who had studied together in Egypt. Both had been members of the Muslim Brotherhood, but broke with the movement over the priority of armed struggle. For about seven years, the organisation engaged in military activities against Israeli army personnel and settlers in Gaza, without however developing a separate armed wing. During the same period, a group of Islamist activists associated with Fatah were operating in the West Bank under the name *Saraya al-Jihad al-Islami*. From 1988 on, Fathi Shiqaqi started to work on the merger of both organisations and the development of standing military structures for the Islamic Jihad. It would however take four more years until *Saraya al-Quds* emerged. Islamic Jihad sources say that the military wing was officially established in 1992 by Mahmoud al-Khawaja '*to replace the different unorganised, individual groups.*'[27] *Saraya al-Quds* also claim to have introduced suicide operations into the Palestinian theatre.

Although the Jihad preceded Hamas by seven years, it has remained the smaller of the two Islamist organisations. Whereas Hamas became a political movement with a strong popular support base and an extensive religious and welfare network, the focus of the Jihad has been on military action instead of political activity. In other words, the Jihad is still very much a revolutionary vanguard; its popular support probably does not exceed five per cent of the Palestinians.

Also, relations between Hamas and Islamic Jihad are shaped by competition; despite various efforts at coordination between the two movements, Hamas has always remained aloof from close cooperation.

Ideology

The ideology of Islamic Jihad differs from Hamas's world view in several ways. Firstly, the Jihad rejects the 'reformist' approach that Hamas inherited from the Muslim Brotherhood. The 'reformist' approach is based on the notion that the Muslim world should tackle the problem of Israel only after a revitalisation of Islam which would do away with its spiritual and religious weakness; as mentioned above, 'Islamisation' is supposed to be achieved through preaching and education. The Jihad, on the contrary, argues that Israel itself is a source of spiritual and religious corruption for Muslims. The Jihad feels that Palestine is the subject of imperialist designs which aim to extend Western control over the Muslim world:

> 'The Zionist entity is the product of the contemporary Western colonisation of the Islamic nation. Its continuing presence on the land of Palestine and in the core of the Islamic nation means a continuing monopoly, partition and dependence imposed by the West on the Islamic nation.'[28]

Therefore Israel has to be confronted directly, immediately and as a means of Islamic spiritual rejuvenation: *'Palestine – "from the river to the sea" – is an Islamic Arab land; the Zionist presence must not be accepted, even if on a little part of Palestine.'*[29] Armed struggle is thus the *raison d'etre* of the Islamic Jihad. This also means that the organisation does not pay any attention to enforcing Islamic values in society.

Secondly, for the Jihad the problem of Palestine cannot solely be framed in nationalistic terms: it is essentially an Islamic issue. Solving the Palestinian question is the key to *'every serious strategy to liberate and unify the Islamic nation.'*[30] In other words, the notion of liberation of Palestine and pan-Islamic revival are closely interlinked and conditional upon each other.

Thirdly, the Islamic Jihad – although a Sunni movement – combines Palestinian Islamic nationalism with the teachings of Ayatollah Khomeini, the Shiite leader of the Iranian Islamic revolution. As laid out by Fathi Shiqaqi in his paper *'Khomeini: al-Hal al-Islami wal-Badil'* in 1979, Khomeini is seen as an exemplary leader for having for the first time given the Palestine question an appropriate place in Islamist ideology, for having dealt a major defeat to the West through the Islamic revolution, and for having successfully established an Islamic state.

Mission and Strategy

Saraya al-Quds is the Islamic Jihad's tool of '*military jihad and attack against Zionist objectives and interests.*'[31] The objectives of armed struggle are defined as follows:

- 'The liberation of all Palestine, the end of the Zionist presence, and the establishment of Islamic rule over the land of Palestine which guarantees justice, freedom and equality.
- The mobilisation of the Palestinian people and the organisation of the population based on a military, political and jihadi stand, with all educational and organisational tools to fulfil its jihadi duties towards Palestine.
- Mobilisation of the Muslim people around the world so that they play their historic role in the battle against the Zionist entity.
- Unification of Islamic efforts towards liberating Palestine and consolidation of relationships with Islamic movements and other freedom fighter movements around the world.'[32]

In its military efforts, *Saraya al-Quds* targets Israeli combatants and civilians. However, attacks on Israeli civilians are seen as a default option and a response to Israeli military action:

> 'We do not support targeting civilians unless provoked by the Israeli army. We would rather engage in a purely military conflict but have to deviate from this in the light of violence against Palestinian civilians.'[33]

The Jihad is currently rethinking its strategic orientation, especially in the light of Hamas' electoral victories of 2005 and 2006. The signals coming from the organisation are mixed. Islamic Jihad officially agreed to the *tahdi'a* of March 2005 but *Saraya al-Quds* has conducted five major suicide bombings in Israel since then. The organisation interprets this as commensurate with the principle of reciprocity in the event of Israeli attacks on its commanders and cadres which was included in the March 2005 'Cairo Agreement': '*The truce does not mean the end, if the Israelis attack us then we have the right to react, this was a condition at the Cairo dialogue which led to the truce.*'[34] Also, since the beginning of 2006 *Saraya al-Quds* has intensified the launching of rockets at Israeli targets from Gaza. On the other hand, political leaders of the organisation have indicated willingness to compromise on various occasions.[35]

The Islamic Jihad has long been sharply critical of the PNA which it refused to recognise. However, unlike Hamas, the organisation did not try to challenge the PNA and Fatah on the political front. Nevertheless, the crackdowns on the Jihad by the Authority, such as in the aftermath of the 1990s suicide bombings in Israel[36], had a comparatively strong impact, given the small size of the organisation. Attitudes towards the PNA are thus split among the members of *Saraya al-Quds*. Whereas some members see the PNA as a Palestinian institution which differs from other Arab regimes, others have a much more confrontational attitude, perceiving the PNA as a pro-American and pro-Israeli regime.[37]

Strength, Equipment and Tactics

Saraya al-Quds has between 1,000 and 2,000 operatives; most estimates put its strength at around 1,600. The majority of the rank-and-file are young males between 18 and 24, mostly refugees from rural areas, except for Gaza. During the second *Intifada*, *Saraya al-Quds* managed to recruit a significant number of Fatah militants and members of the PNA security apparatuses, mainly in the northern West Bank. While *Saraya al-Quds* recruits do not have to follow the same strict education programme as *Izz ad-Din al-Qassam* operatives, they do receive an ideological and military training which is deemed sufficient for[38] operational readiness.

Like *Izz ad-Din al-Qassam*, *Saraya al-Quds* is equipped with M-16/M-4 and AK-47 assault rifles, RPG launchers, and mortars, as well as the home-produced *Al-Quds* rocket, which is equivalent to the *Al-Qassam*. Efforts have been made to procure longer-range Russian-type *Grad* missile (about 20 kilometres range, with a 14-kilogram warhead) from Hizbullah. *Saraya al-Quds* use shootings, suicide-bombings and rockets. The organisation has proved fairly resilient in the face of Israeli counter-insurgency measures and innovative in terms of tactics.[39]

Saraya al-Quds has its strongholds in Gaza and the northern West Bank, in particular Tulkarem and Jenin. The outbreak of the second *Intifada* gave a boost to the organisation. During the height of confrontation, *Saraya al-Quds* carried out several joint operations with the *Al-Aqsa Martyrs Brigades*. Fewer joint activities were carried out with Hamas' military wing which views *Saraya al-Quds* as a competitor.[40]

Command and Control

Saraya al-Quds operates in small cells without central command. Since 2005, Israel has waged an intense military campaign against the organisation and killed or arrested many senior commanders in the northern West Bank and Gaza. However, *Saraya al-Quds* managed to recover and has maintained operational capacity, with lost cadres being replaced relatively quickly.

The political leadership of the Islamic Jihad – namely Secretary-General Ramadan Shallah and the policy-making *Shoura* Council – is based in Damascus; inside the Palestinian Territories, the organisation has less political infrastructure, with Khaled al-Batsh as the official spokesman. It is not entirely clear to what extent the political wing exerts operational control over actions on the ground. For instance, the fact that *Saraya al-Quds* has continued with suicide bombings during the *tahdi'a* is partly explained as the result of splits within the leadership towards the benefits of a truce.

Since the Israeli deportation of Islamic Jihad founders Fathi Shiqaqi and Abd al-Aziz Awda to Lebanon in 1988, the organisation has enjoyed close ties with Hizbullah and Iran. With the support of Hizbullah, the Jihad managed to expand its network in the Palestinian refugee camps in Lebanon. Although often described as an instrument of Iranian foreign policy towards Israel, *Saraya al-Quds* adamantly maintains that it is an autonomous organisation:

'Saraya al-Quds believes in cooperation with Hizbullah and Iran, as well as the International Islamic Jihad Organisation. We received support, and there is ongoing cooperation on different levels but there is independence in the operations, in other words Iran does not influence our tactics or strategy.'[41]

Financing

Iran is the main financial sponsor, whereas Hizbullah provides training, armament and logistical support. Yet, determining the exact amount of financial support to *Saraya al-Quds* is quite difficult, with accounts varying widely. The most common estimate is of some $2 million per year.

Al-Aqsa Martyrs Brigades (Kata'ib Shuhada' al-Aqsa)

The *Al-Aqsa Martyrs Brigades* are the military arm of the Palestinian National Liberation Movement, Fatah (reverse acronym of *Harakat al-Tahrir al-Watani al-Filastini*). They were one of the driving forces behind the second *Intifada*. The *Brigades* emerged shortly after the outbreak of the uprising in September 2000 and were founded by a cluster of Fatah activists in the Balata refugee camp in Nablus, many of them 'graduates' of the first *Intifada*. The Brigades claim the killing of a Jewish settler near the West Bank village of Jalameh at the beginning of 2001 as their first operation. The *Brigades* see themselves as the '*protective wing of the Palestinian people.*'[42]

In many respects, the *Al-Aqsa Brigades* were a local response by grassroots Fatah activists who feared that their movement would lose legitimacy and popular support to Hamas and Islamic Jihad in the course of the *Intifada*. With the main powerhouse located in Nablus and Ramallah, *Brigades* soon emerged in Jenin, Tulkarem and Bethlehem, as well as in Gaza.[43] Some of these groups then turned into militias gathered around local strongmen, such as the *Martyr Abu Rish Brigades* in the central Gaza Strip and the *Jenin Martyrs Brigades* in the Bureij refugee camp. Other sub-groupings are the *Mujahidin Brigades*, the *Al-Fatah al-Mubin Brigades* or the *Fursan al-Asifa Brigades*. Much of the *Brigades'* infrastructure and funds derive from the Fatah *tanzim*, the movement's political organisation at grassroots level.

Ideology

The *Al-Aqsa Brigades* claim to be faithful to Fatah's ideology of confrontation with Israel as a means to establishing a Palestinian state. They view armed struggle as the preferred way to achieve their goals: an independent Palestinian state in the West Bank and Gaza with Jerusalem as its capital, based on a full Israeli withdrawal to the pre-1967 borders, the evacuation of all settlements and the right of return for all refugees. This state is to have full political and security control over people and territory.[44] The *Brigades* describe themselves as being in the lineage of previous Fatah armed groups, such *Al-Asifa* and the *Fatah Hawks*, which were active during the first *Intifada*.

The ideology of the *Brigades* is based on Palestinian nationalism, not Islamism. In other words, the *Brigades* are a secular group. However, over the past years they have partly adopted religious rhetoric and symbols and share with Islamist factions the perception of the '*US-Israeli occupation of Palestine.*'[45]

Mission and Strategy

The *Al-Aqsa Brigades* use military means to achieve the goals of establishing an independent Palestinian state. In comparison to *Izz ad-Din al-Qassam* and *Saraya al-Quds*, the *Brigades* have refrained from issuing sophisticated communiqués explaining their mission and strategy, partly because they identify themselves as implementing the political goals of Fatah.

In terms of strategy, the *Brigades* initially limited their activities to targeting Israeli military personnel and settlers in the West Bank and Gaza. Then, from early 2002 they undertook armed operations against civilians inside Israel. However, the *Brigades* witnessed various splits and divisions which make it difficult to talk about a united strategy. In March 2005, they accepted the PNA-sponsored *tahdi'a* and ceased all operations. The *Brigades* also embarked on a process of integration into the PNA security organisations which was initiated by Mohammad Dahlan, the former Gaza head of the *Preventive Security* and Minister of Civilian Affairs. As one senior activist explains:

> 'The Brigades are committed to the PNA policy of creation of a suitable atmosphere to resume the peace process and to avoid giving Israel excuses to continue its harsh policy of repression against the Palestinians and their authority.'[46]

Relations between the *Brigades* and the Fatah-controlled PNA are complex and hard to pin down. Leaders and militants of the groups regularly identify themselves with Fatah, although Fatah officials often denied recognising that they were the military wing of the movement. A senior operative characterises the links as follows:

> 'The relationship with the PNA is normal, and we are in continuous touch with President Abbas to learn about the latest developments. The PNA has absorbed the Brigades into its security apparatuses.'[47]

During the *Intifada*, the *Al-Aqsa Brigades* were working with Islamist militant organisations in the West Bank and Gaza Strip.[48] This cooperation included the sharing of information and technical know-how, as well as the formation of so-called 'cocktail cells'. In general, the *Brigades* found it easier to work with *Saraya al-Quds* due to its lack of ideological requirements, but in some areas there were also good relations with *Izz ad-Din al-Qassam*. Kinship relations between militants of various organisations often facilitated joint action.

Strength, Equipment and Tactics

The *Brigades* are comprised of some 800 full-time operatives, many of them so-called 'wanted men' (operatives wanted by the Israeli security forces), and some 4,000 part-time activists and supporters. Many members are young males – between 18 and 24 years old – from the refugee camps in the West Bank and Gaza. Some 30 per cent of *Brigades* operatives are members of the PNA security organisations, which have long been dominated by Fatah, in particular *Preventive Security* and *General Intelligence*. *Brigades* leaders claim that they could easily have increased their manpower in terms of recruits but were forced to forego this due to the lack of capacity.[49]

Like the other Palestinian armed groups, the *Brigades* are equipped with M-16/M-4 and AK-47 assault rifles and RPG launchers. Their variants of the *Qassam* rocket are called *Aqsa* (in reference to the *Al-Aqsa* Mosque in Jerusalem) or *Asifa* ('Storm'). The *Brigades* have used suicide bombings, car bombings, kidnappings, shootings and knife attacks against Israeli soldiers and civilians; they are also engaged in the shooting of collaborators. In terms of tactics, they went through various changes: at the beginning of the *Intifada*, the *Brigades* lacked the capabilities to carry out the 'professional' bombings which were the trademark of the Islamist groups. Thus they confined themselves to shooting attacks on IDF personnel and settlers travelling on the West Bank roads, as well as occasionally on civilians inside Israel. In January 2002, the *Brigades* then began to carry out suicide bombings in Israel, employing unusual tactics such as the use of female suicide operatives.

Command and Control

The *Brigades'* structure is that of a loose network of cells in the main West Bank and Gaza cities. These cells – so-called 'military units' – are responsible for carrying out attacks and providing internal security for the groups. *Brigades* leaders have underlined that their loose organisational set-up made Israeli counter-insurgency measures difficult:

> 'The formation of small local groups by the Brigades made it more difficult for the Israelis to capture us. Any infiltration of Hamas' well-organised military structures was deadly and led to the exposure of all cell members in a specific area.'[50]

The localised character of the *Brigades* is reinforced by a loose, personality-driven command structure. In fact, the *Brigades* never had any central or unified command and control. Operational decisions are taken by the cells themselves:

> 'Every group or cell of the Brigades has the freedom to decide when and where to carry out attacks against suitable or possible targets. Decision-making is with local leaders. When the IDF assassinates a senior commander, any group which has the capability to retaliate will do so. Nobody needs to tell them what to do.'[51]

Brigades groupings in Nablus have sometimes claimed to function as a central command post, but these claims rather express a bid for legitimacy than actual control. At the beginning of the *Intifada*, West Bank Fatah leader Marwan Barghouti, currently imprisoned by Israel, provided some guidance and support to the *Brigades*, again however without exercising effective control.

In fact, Fatah as an organisation never had a grip on the *Brigades'* decision-making. On the contrary, command and control in the *Brigades* soon became a function of financial and material patronage by certain individuals in the PNA security organisations or local Fatah leaders; the latter often use the *Brigades* as a means of obtaining political influence. *Brigades* leaders regularly complain about this phenomenon:

> 'For a while in 2001, we succeeded in creating a central command for the Brigades – from Rafah in the south to Jenin in the north – to coordinate between political and military activities and to avoid chaos in structure and operations. But the [PNA] security commanders and the Fatah movement undermined these efforts. I can say that Fatah splits and division were always reflected in the Brigades.'[52]

The fragmentation of decision-making and the localised character of the *Brigades* also led to increasing interference in social and economic life after the armed groups were driven underground by the IDF in 2002. Many senior commanders, such as Nasr Awais, Mahmud Titi or Raed Karmi, were killed or captured by Israel and replaced by younger commanders who started to engage in illegal activities in order to secure funding. In many areas, the lines between military resistance and criminal activity have thus become blurred. In 2005 and 2006, elements of the *Brigades* were also involved in the kidnapping of foreigners in Gaza.

Financing

The *Al-Aqsa Brigades* have various sources of funding. Until 2004, the late PNA President Yasser Arafat financed some *Brigades* groupings through Fouad Shobaki, a PNA financial official and close adviser. However, these financial contributions were made to coopt and control the *Brigades* rather than to enable them to carry out operations.[53]

As Fatah refused to provide systematic and continued funding, the *Brigades* had to find other ways of financial support:

> 'We needed the sponsorship and the support from the Fatah movement but they ran away from their responsibility during our war with the Israelis. Fatah's rejection pushed us to seek external finance to keep our activities going on.'[54]

In some cases, Fatah officials from inside or outside the Palestinian Territories paid *Brigades* groupings from their own pockets, such as Munir Maqdeh (Abu Hassan), Fatah military commander in Tyre in Lebanon. Other *Brigades* elements received funds from Islamic Jihad, Hizbullah and Iran, especially in the northern West Bank. Operational activity increasingly became a function of external financial support:

> 'Some of our groups got money from Iran, Hizbullah and the Islamic Jihad. Hizbullah is a resistance organisation, which is fighting the same enemy, and it is normal that revolutionary organisations support each other, but this finance should not affect our policy. Unfortunately, the Iranians and Hizbullah wanted us to move in their path, and the Iranian Intelligence and the Revolutionary Guards pressured us and the Islamic Jihad to carry out attacks, or they would stop the funding.'[55]

In summer and autumn 2005, the *Brigades* were largely put on the payroll of the PNA security services.

Nasser Salah ad-Din Brigades ('Alwiyat an-Nasir Salah ad-Din)

The *Nasser Salah ad-Din Brigades* are the military wing of the Popular Resistance Committees (PRCs). They share various characteristics with the *Al-Aqsa Brigades*, such as personalised decision-making, dependence on patronage and lack of ideological sophistication. The PRCs, an umbrella structure for militants of various factions, are based in Gaza and have only a minimal presence in the West Bank. Jamal Abu Samhadana, a former Fatah official from Rafah, created the organisation at the beginning of the second *Intifada*.

Ideology

Since its operatives stem from different political backgrounds, the PRCs had to develop a set of principles which constitute something of a lowest common denominator. Leaders of the PRCs state that the group prefers military action to ideological commitments:

> 'In our actions, we do not attempt to follow a specific ideology. Every Jihad activist in the Popular Resistance Committees and its military wing, the Nasser Salah ad-Din Brigades, must carry out his duty to his nation and his homeland, without regard to any ideology or commitment to a specific organisation.'[56]

Adherence to Islam is a key principle for the PRCs: 'We believe in the source of our heritage, and our Islamic belief carries a heavenly message to the *whole of humanity.*'[57] However, the commitment to Islam is rather general and seen mainly as a source of motivation and psychological preparation for the struggle: '*The Islamic viewpoint for the conflict with Israel provided us with the strength of the Islamic faith which opposes the humiliation caused by a conqueror.*'[58] As opposed to Hamas, the PRCs do not pay any attention to the social issues or advocate any specific Islamic agenda. Also, the PRCs do not frame the conflict with Israel in religious terms like the Islamic Jihad does: '*We do not suggest that the war between us and our enemy will turn into a religious war, since we do not fight the Jews because they are Jewish, but because they conquered and stole our land.*'[59] However, the PRCs do understand armed struggle against Israel as their most important task. Resistance is seen as the only way to end the occupation and free all Palestine: '*We support any Jihad act on any conquered land against every settler that has stolen our land. We do not distinguish between 1967 and 1948.*'[60]

Mission and Strategy

Apart from national liberation, the PRCs have no long-term goals as they were formed in answer to an immediate situation, namely the second *Intifada*. The Committees work on two fronts, mobilisation of the Palestinian population for armed struggle through what they call the 'popular branch' and military training and activities.[61] The *Nasser Salah ad-Din Brigades* aim to translate the umbrella concept of the PRCs into practical cooperation with other armed groups on the ground: '*We are unified in the field both in public and military action. In these two aspects the unity between the organisations has been in the actual military operations.*'[62] To this effect, the *Salah ad-Din Brigades* closely coordinate their actions with *Izz ad-Din al-Qassam* and, to a lesser extent, with *Saraya al-Quds*. Close personal relations exist between members of the PRCs and PNA security personnel such as from the *Preventive Security*, especially in southern Gaza. However, in other areas relations between the PRCs and the PNA security organisations have been tense.

Strength, Equipment and Tactics

The *Salah ad-Din Brigades* have an estimated strength of some 500 operatives and are divided into three branches for southern, central and northern Gaza. The personnel is composed of former Fatah officials, members of PNA security organisations, Hamas operatives, Jihad operatives, as well as PFLP and DFLP militants. Many of them originate from the Gaza refugee camps, especially Jabaliya, Shati, and Rafah. Between those activists there are long-standing personal relations that date back to the first *Intifada*.[63]

Like other militant groups, the *Salah ad-Din Brigades* are equipped with M16/M-4 and AK-47 assault rifles, RPG launchers, and mortars, as well as the *Nasser* rocket, their version of the *Al-Qassam* rocket. Their tactics include shootings and high-trajectory fire with mortars and rockets against IDF personnel and Israeli civilians. The *Salah ad-Din Brigades* have developed considerable expertise in the use of IED (Improvised Explosive Devices) and managed to destroy three Israeli *Merkava* tanks with roadside bombs in Gaza. The *Brigades* are also active against collaborators and domestic opponents and claimed responsibility for the killing of Moussa Arafat, nephew of the late PNA President and Head of the *Military Intelligence* in September 2005. The organisation is also said to have been involved in the bomb attack on a US diplomatic convoy in northern Gaza in October 2003.

Command and Control

The *Salah ad-Din Brigades* have a personalised command structure and operated under the orders of its founder, Jamal Abu Samhadana. However, Samhadana was assassinated by Israel in 2006, as was his successor Abu Yussef Al-Qoqa. It has been contended that the *Brigades* have come strongly under the influence of *Izz ad-Din al-Qassam* and have served as a proxy for Hamas' military activities during the *tahdi'a*; however, conclusive evidence for this has still to be presented.

Financing

The *Salah ad-Din Brigades* receive funding through illegal activities and external patronage. Members of the organisation control the smuggling of goods, weapons and ammunition from Egypt, either through tunnels under the Gaza-Egypt borders or across the Mediterranean sea. The *Brigades* also receive funding from other Palestinian factions, as well as from external sources such as Hizbullah and Iran.

Dealing with Non-Statutory Armed Groups

A Challenge to Security Sector Governance?

Since the outbreak of the *Intifada*, Palestinian non-statutory armed groups have gained additional political prominence. This has been primarily due to the decreasing capacity of the PNA to uphold law and order. In the ensuing security vacuum, a patchwork of localised authorities has emerged. The Israeli policy of geographical fragmentation and cantonisation accelerated this trend. In such an environment, political power has often become a function of guns and money rather than ideology.

In this perspective, non-statutory armed groups have become an integral part of Palestinian security sector governance. According to a poll by DCAF and the Graduate Institute of Development Studies of the University of Geneva (IUED), Palestinians place significantly higher trust in non-statutory armed groups than in the PNA security organisations. According to the survey, the *Izz ad-Din al-Qassam Brigades* and the *Al-Aqsa Brigades* are the most trusted security actors in the Palestinian Territories: 34 per cent of the interviewees had great trust in the *Al-Qassam Brigades*, and 29 per cent had great trust in the *Al-Aqsa Brigades*, as opposed to 21 per cent in the *Civil Police* and 18 per cent in the *Preventive Security*.[64]

Despite their rather positive public perception, the existence of nonstatutory security actors outside the PNA framework poses a variety of political and social challenges. Firstly, from an institutional perspective, non-statutory armed groups might further undermine what little is left in terms of legitimacy for the PNA. In some areas, armed groups have already effectively taken over the monopoly on the use of force and function as parallel, localised governments. Also, armed groups are partly being used by powerful individuals or external actors to advance their own interests, at the expense of the common good. If these trends continue, they might well lead to a Somalia-style scenario, with all central authority vanished and warlords fighting over power and funds. Various developments in spring 2006 point in such a direction, such as the fierce clashes in Gaza between the *Preventive Security* and *Izz ad-Din al-Qassam*.

Secondly, although armed groups enjoy significant popular support and legitimacy, they have increasingly come to combine paramilitary action with interference in societal affairs. For instance, non-state armed groups are involved in dispute-resolution and adjudication. Whereas this might have positive results in some cases, in other cases the dividing line between resistance, law and order and criminal activity is not so clear. Armed groups have repeatedly engaged in extortion, blackmailing, armed assaults and theft of property.

Thirdly, the activities of armed groups have often brought harm and damage to the Palestinian civilian population. This has been the case directly, for instance through the mishandling of weapons and explosives or misguided rocket fire; it has also been the case indirectly through provoking Israeli military operations that harm the civilian population in the area. Furthermore, non-statutory groups have contributed to the spread of arms in Palestinian society.

Finally, the actions of non-statutory armed groups also have a direct impact on the 'peace process', or what is left of it. Continued armed operations by Palestinian resistance factions, such as rocket fire from Gaza or suicide bombings against civilians inside Israel, have regularly put the PNA in a tight spot vis-à-vis the international community. This made it easy for Israel to claim that there is no Palestinian partner who would be willing or able to dismantle what it calls the 'terrorist infrastructure.'

Strategic Options

Irrespective of how non-statutory armed groups and their activities are perceived by the Palestinians, it is reasonable to assume that the current process of political and institutional fragmentation in the PNA runs counter to long-term aspirations of statebuilding. If Palestinians want to build strong and effective institutions, they need to agree on the political and organisational future of nonstatutory armed groups. This is not to exclude the importance of Israeli policies and the obstacles posed by the continuing occupation to any form of Palestinian governance. But if Palestinians feel that they want to continue on the path of institutionalising whatever gains have been made since the inception of the *Oslo* process, the issue of strengthening the PNA as the central authority in the Palestinian Territories can hardly be avoided.

Should the Palestinians decide to address the issue of non-statutory armed groups, three options are available to them: forced disarmament, voluntary demilitarisation, and integration into the PNA security infrastructure.

Option 1: Forced Disarmament: Regional and international actors have always been in favour of the forced disarmament of Palestinian armed groups and have supported like-minded Palestinians. Coercive disarmament is commonly directed against the Islamist groups and would have to be implemented by the PNA security forces.

However, after clashes between Hamas and Fatah resulted in the defeat of the PNA security forces in Gaza and the takeover of all security installations by Hamas, the option has lost its attractiveness. Hamas' military wing has proved to be better trained, equipped and structured than the official security forces, despite all the training and equipment that the *Presidential Guard*, the *National Security Forces* and the *Preventive Security* had received. The *Izz ad-Din al-Qassam Brigades* are highly motivated and have a higher troop morale. Moreover, Islamist groups, particularly Hamas, had managed to infiltrate operatives into the lower and middle ranks of various security organisations.

The bloodshed during the confrontation in 2007 illustrated what could have happened if PNA security organisations had attempted to disarm Islamist groups. In view of what occurred in Gaza and the rising strength of Hamas, Palestinian leaders may hesitate to repeat the experience in the West Bank, although the balance of power there is more favourable to the Fatah-dominated security forces. Public opinion in the Arab world would perceive such action as instigated by Israel and the United States.

Also, forced disarmament by the PNA would be unlikely to be directed against the various groups operating under the umbrella of the *Al-Aqsa Brigades*, due to the fact that they are an offshoot of Fatah, with many operatives simultaneously serving in the

PNA security forces. However, it is the *Al-Aqsa Brigades* that have interfered particularly in Palestinian daily life, not so much the better disciplined *Izz ad-Din Al-Qassam* and *Saraya al-Quds*.

Option 2: Voluntary Demilitarisation: Voluntary demilitarisation would mean that the armed groups decommission their arms and dismantle themselves by their own decision. It is easy to see that such an option is equally unlikely to be taken. Firstly, no Palestinian group would give up the 'arms of resistance' in the face of the unabated conflict with Israel; any such move would be perceived as surrender to the enemy and clash with the ethos of 'steadfast resistance.' Also, recent history, particularly the on-going Israeli campaign of arrests and targeted assassinations and the experience of the ill-fated *hudna* of 2003, have proven to the Islamist groups that Israeli military activities against them are likely to continue.

Secondly, organisational interests militate against the option of voluntary demilitarisation. For the Islamist organisations, the dismantling of their military wings would be akin to giving up their most important political card and their main tool of recruitment. Possibly, it would mean losing major sources of external funding from actors who have an interest in the continuation of the conflict. As to the *Al-Aqsa Brigades* and the PRCs there are many operatives for whom armed activity is the only source of income; also, some mid-level and senior commanders have discovered that the 'war economy' upon which they thrive provides considerable financial benefits. Finally, for some groups, in particular *Saraya al-Quds* and *Izz ad-Din al-Qassam*, there are also ideological imperatives for the continuation of armed struggle.

Option 3: Integration into the PNA Security Infrastructure: The integration of non-statutory armed groups into the PNA security infrastructure, coupled with partial demobilisation, would mean that personnel of the various armed factions would join the PNA security branches individually or as a group. For those unwilling to join the security branches other means of employment would have to be found.

A process along these lines would have to comprise political and technical elements. Addressing the root causes of a conflict and creating a political horizon for non-statutory armed groups are generally preconditions for disarmament. In the Palestinian case, these conditions are absent and unlikely to be fulfilled in the near future, given Israel's declared intent to stick with its strategy of 'unilateralism.' However, what could be achieved is to include armed groups and their mother movements formally into the Palestinian political system and give them a stake in the national institutions, notably the PNA and the PLO (Palestine Liberation Organisation). This would require careful negotiations centring on the political future of their members and inter-factional consensus on the definition of Palestinian security.

Palestinian non-statutory armed groups have developed different positions toward political inclusion. Hamas has clearly undergone the most radical shift in this regard, taking into account its long-standing refusal to participate in the *Oslo* framework. With the 2006 legislative elections, Hamas has not only become part of the PNA but in fact assumed control of large parts of it. Hamas has mostly stuck to the *tahdi'a* and offered to embark on a long-term *hudna* with Israel upon the assumption of governmental responsibility.[65] With regard to the PRCs, the organisation is quite likely to follow the position of Hamas, given its political and personal affinity to the movement.

Islamic Jihad takes a more ambivalent position. The organisation is currently in the process of recalibrating its stance towards political inclusion. It has not participated in the 2006 elections but also not prevented its supporters from going to the polls. In fact, integration into the PLO might be easier to achieve, as the Jihad has no intention of outmuscling Fatah on the political front, as is the case with Hamas. Increased popular support for Islamic Jihad which has developed in the course of the 2006 stand-off between Fatah and Hamas might also contribute to a certain moderation in its position towards the PNA.

The *Al-Aqsa Brigades* would be a slightly different case. They represent the position of a major political player, Fatah, are organisationally closer to the PNA and more receptive to material incentives. Here the problem lies more in ensuring compliance with political agreements, given their decentralised decision-making structure and competing sources of patronage.

On the operational level, the integration process would centre on the organisational inclusion of operatives into the various PNA security organisations. This would involve the training and/or rehabilitation of militants, adequate salaries to guarantee their livelihoods and the control or transfer of their weapons. Militants unwilling to join the security organisations might be offered access to training, education or job creation programmes.

Effective depoliticisation of the PNA security branches would be an important condition for the integration process to succeed. As long as Fatah continues to dominate the security organisations and as long as they are perceived as unprofessional and partisan, incentives will be high for Hamas to maintain the *Executive Force* as a security organisation under its exclusive control.

Past experiences with the integration of militants might prove useful here. In early 2005, PNA President Abbas ordered the *Al-Aqsa Brigades* to merge with the official PNA security branches. Various schemes of rehabilitation were introduced, and almost all *Brigades* militants were either placed on the security payroll or given monthly allowances, though only some of the *Brigades* operatives actually work in the security forces.

Hamas has also shown some flexibility in recent years. Since 2005, Hamas has repeatedly called for the establishment of a Palestinian army which would merge all Palestinian factions into one organisation. Moreover, in 2003 Hamas operatives were temporarily included in the local PNA security structure in Hebron. Close kinship or personal relations between militants from various factions, as well as between militants and PNA security personnel could be a facilitating factor in this regard. The establishment of the *Executive Force* was not only intended to ward off pressure from Fatah, but also to find employment for members of *Izz ad-Din al-Qassam* who have had little engagement in armed activity since March 2005. The *Executive Force* can be seen as a first step by Hamas towards reorienting its military capacities from resistance activity towards law and order functions and might constitute an entry point for longer-term disarmament.

As an option, integration can only be seriously contemplated when the political and economic conditions are in place. But even then, integration carries several risks. The fragmented command and control structure of the PNA might further disintegrate under the pressure created by conflicting organisational cultures and varying attitudes to discipline that the members of armed groups would bring to the PNA. Members of Islamist groups might also radicalise the PNA security organisations and create internal tensions.

This could expose the PNA and its security infrastructure to renewed Israeli targeting. It is also not clear how the PNA might afford financially the integration of large numbers of militants in the absence of increased internal revenues or donor aid; the latter in particular might be difficult to attain if it is perceived as funding 'terrorists.' Finally, the dire economic situation in the Palestinian Territories makes it unlikely that demobilised militants will find a secure income in high numbers.

Conclusion

As of summer 2007, prospects for finding a Palestinian consensus on how to deal with non-statutory armed groups appear rather mixed. On the positive side, the most important armed Palestinian faction, Hamas, has shown considerable flexibility in political and military terms over the past two years. The landslide victory scored by the movement in the Palestinian legislative elections has provided an important opportunity to build on this record of flexibility. History shows that the inclusion of armed groups in political processes tends to moderate their behaviour, especially in relation to the use of violence. Not surprisingly, Hamas has largely halted its armed activities and repeatedly offered a long-term ceasefire with Israel.

However, on the negative side, Hamas's victory and the subsequent reaction by Fatah have led to a situation of stark domestic tension, particularly on the elite-level and between the followers of both movements. The US and Israel, with the active support of the EU, have pursued a strategy of regime change with the objective of removing Hamas from power. These massive external interferences and the international economic boycott made the work of Hamas in government extremely difficult and reduced the incentives for the movement to dismantle or integrate its military wing. On the other side, new sources of patronage have boosted the role of the *Al-Aqsa Brigades.*

It is too early to see where these dynamics will lead in the future and how they will influence non-state armed groups. It remains uncertain whether it will stimulate further fragmentation and warlordism that could eventually offer *Al-Qaeda* a foothold in the Palestinian arena, or whether the cohesive power of the Palestinian national movement is still strong enough to find a consensus. What seems evident however is that the window of opportunity provided by the ascent of Hamas to power is rapidly closing.

Notes

1   Statutory security actors can be understood as comprising all organisations with the official mandate to use force in a state framework. This includes armed forces, police, paramilitary forces, gendarmeries, civilian and military intelligence services, and border guards. Nonstatutory security actors then comprise liberation and guerrilla armies, political party and private militias, as well as private security companies.

2   Due to their limited military capacities, the armed wings of the Popular Front for the Liberation of Palestine (PFLP), the *Martyr Abu Ali Mustafa Brigades*, and the Democratic Front for the Liberation of Palestine (DFLP), the *National Resistance Brigades*, are not included here.

3   The 'war of the knives' referred to a campaign of knive attacks by Hamas activists against Israeli soldiers and civilians in autumn 1990, following the killing of 22 Palestinians by the Israeli army in the vicinity of the Al-Aqsa Mosque in Jerusalem in October 1990.

4   Sheikh Shehada was killed by Israel in 2002.

5   Yet it is important to note that Hamas as a movement emphasises social and political action over theological reasoning. Hamas gives less importance to scholarly sophistication than, for instance, the Islamic Jihad.

6   See Khaled Hroub, *Hamas. Political Thought and Practice*, Institute for Palestine Studies, Washington 2000, pp. 43-68.

7   *The Charter of Allah: The Platform of the Islamic Resistance Movement (Hamas), Article 11.*

8   *Islamic Resistance Movement (Hamas) Introductory Memorandum*, p. 5.

9   Ibid.

10 Ibid.

11 Ibid.

12 *Hamas, Periodic Statement No. 10*, 12 March 1988.

13 Here Hamas speaks about '*the liberation of Palestine and the return of the Palestinian People to its independent state with its capital Jerusalem*', without specifying the geographical scope of such an 'independent state.' Change and Reform Platform, First Paragraph.

14 The 'Prisoner's Document' is a political platform agreed upon by five Palestinian faction leaders in Israeli detention, representing Fatah, Hamas, Islamic Jihad, PFLP and DFLP. The document calls for the establishment of an '*independent state with al-Quds al-Shareef as its capital on all territories occupied in 1967, and to secure the right of return for refugees to their homes and properties from which they were evicted and to compensate them.*' National Conciliation Document of the Palestinian Prisoners, 28 June 2006.

15 *Charter of Allah, Article 7*. The group took its name from Sheikh Izz ad-Din al-Qassam, a Syrian-born Palestinian insurgent leader, who was killed in 1935 by the British in the Jenin area in the northern West Bank.

16 http://www.alqassam.ps/english/aboutus.htm

17 Ibid.

18 '*If an enemy invades Muslim territories, then Jihad and fighting the enemy becomes an individual duty on every Muslim.*' Charter of Allah, Article 12.

19 *Memorandum from the Islamic Resistance Movement (Hamas) to the Kings, Presidents, and Ministers Meeting at Sharm al-Sheikh*, 13 March 1996.

20 In February 1994, the Israeli settler Baruch Goldstein killed 29 praying Palestinians in the Hebron shrine.

21 *Izz ad-Din al-Qassam* in the West Bank have traditionally had their centres in the Hebron and Nablus areas.

22 http://www.alqassam.ps/english/aboutus.htm.

23 Interview with senior Hamas operative, January 2006.

24 http://www.alqassam.ps/english/aboutus.htm. With the fall of dozens of commanders and many field operatives since 2001, *Izz ad-Din al-Qassam* expanded their activities to supporting families of former activists through a charitable trust.

25 Such was the case for example in October 2005 when Hamas responded to an explosion during a parade in Jabalia, in which 19 Palestinians were killed, with a volley of *Qassam* rockets on Israel.

26 The best example of 'renegade' behaviour was the 19 August 2003 suicide bombing on the No. 2 bus in Jerusalem which killed 23 civilians and brought the 2003 *hudna* to an end. This operation was carried out by a former Islamic Jihad member who belonged to a small tight-knit group of Jihad and Hamas militants in Hebron which was unknown to either leadership.

27 Interview with a senior military commander of the Islamic Jihad in the West Bank, October 2005.

28 'Nabasa 'an Haraka al-Jihad al-Islami fi Filastin', www.qudsway.com. See also http: //www. qudsnews.net/top009.asp. (Accessed 31 May 2006)

29 Ibid.

30 Ibid.

31 'Saraya al-Quds. Al-Jinah al-'Askari lil- Haraka al-Jihad al-Islami fi Filastin', http: //www. sarayaalquds.org/saraya/saraya001.htm (Accessed 26 May 2006)

32 'Nabasa 'an Haraka al-Jihad al-Islami fi Filastin', www.qudsway.com. (Accessed 31 May 2006)

33 Interview with a senior military commander of the Islamic Jihad in the West Bank, October 2005.

34 Ibid.

35 See for example a statement by Abu Qassam, Islamic Jihad political leader in the northern West Bank : '*If Islamic Jihad participates in the Palestinian Authority, and the PA reaches a settlement with Israel, this will be recognition on our part. Not official recognition, but recognition.*' Islamic Jihad: We may recognise the State of Israel', Haaretz, 3 August 2005.

36 In 1996, the PNA rounded up dozens of cadres of *Saraya al-Quds* and tortured them; at least 18 were held in prison for more than eight years. Interview with a senior military commander of the Islamic Jihad in the West Bank, October 2005

37 Interview with a senior military commander of the Islamic Jihad in the West Bank, October 2005.

38 '*For our Mujahideen, the strategy and the goals are clear and cannot be changed. They are unwilling to make any concession regarding the Palestinian cause.*' Ibid.

39 In 2006, various Jihad suicide operatives were officially figuring as and acting like Hamas activists.

40 Generally, the relations among the military wings are much tighter than the relations among the political factions. As a leading member of *Saraya al-Quds* phrases it: '*Every fighter can be arrested by the Israelis, injured, or killed, so as he expects death at any moment, why should he not keep good contacts with the fighters around him?*' (Interview with a senior military commander of the Islamic Jihad in the West Bank, October 2005).

41 Interview with a senior military commander of the Islamic Jihad in the West Bank, October 2005.

42 Interview with senior *Brigades* leader in the West Bank, September 2005.

43 Interview with senior *Brigades* leader in the West Bank, October 2005.

44 Interview with senior *Brigades* leader in the West Bank, September 2005.

45 Ibid.

46 Ibid.

47 Interview with senior *Brigades* leader in the West Bank, October 2005.

48 '*Relations are good. As we consider ourselves part of the Palestinian resistance, the relationship between the Palestinian military groups is much better than it is among the political factions. The field commands gave a good model of cooperation and coordination which also influenced the political factions. This is the opposite of what happened during the first Intifada when the relations between the political factions affected the relations between the military groups.*' Ibid.

49   '*Many youngsters in the Palestinians cities wanted to join. But if we were to absorb more mem-bers, we need more capacities. Due to the shortage in this regard we were unable to expand the Brigades in terms of strength.*' Ibid.

50   Ibid.

51   Ibid.

52   Interview with senior *Brigades* leader in the West Bank, September 2005.

53   '*At the beginning we did not have regular funding. We got some donations to finance our ac-tivities, but our weapons were our own, and the ammunition we got through personal efforts. Then Yasser Arafat provided the Brigades with money to contain them and keep them under his control.*' Ibid.

54   Interview with senior *Brigades* leader in the West Bank, October 2005.

55   Ibid.

56   'Muhammad al-Baba: Al-Muqawama al-Sha'biya al-Filastiniya fauq al-Aidalou hayat', 18 Feb-ruary 2003. http://www.islamonline.net/Arabic/politics/2003/02/article08.shtml. (Accessed 6 April 2006) See also http://www.moqawmh.com/man_nahno.php. (Accessed 6 April 2006)

57   Ibid.

58   Ibid.

59   Ibid.

60   Ibid.

61   http://www.moqawmh.com/man_nahno.php. (Accessed 7 April 2006)

62   'Muhammad al-Baba: Al-Muqawama al-Sha'biya al-Filastiniya fauq al-Aidalou hayat', 18 Feb-ruary 2003. http://www.islamonline.net/Arabic/politics/2003/02/article08.shtml. (Accessed 6 April 2006)

63   '*The youth came to know each other during the years of the first Intifada, a large number of them had been imprisoned before, a large number had been deported overseas and had returned to the Gaza Strip, and a third part knew each other from the positions they held in the various or-ganisations.*' Ibid.

64   Only the *Civil Defence*, the PNA fire-fighters and emergency services, enjoy an equivalent level of high trust (34 per cent). Bocco, R., De Martino, L., Luethold, A., Friedrich, R., *Palestinian Public Perceptions of Security Sector Governance, Summary Report*, DCAF/ IUED, Geneva, 21 November 2005, p. 8.

65   In addition to this, Hamas has ostensibly run on a platform of good governance and anticorrup-tion for which it is likely to be held accountable by the Palestinian people.

The Challenge for Hamas:
Establishing Transparency and Accountability

Ghazi Ahmad Hamad

Prior to the Palestinian elections of 25 January 2006, Hamas had not been expecting at all that it would suddenly find itself in a position to govern. Until the last moment, the movement had anticipated winning only some 25 seats. It had not hoped for more, but simply to become a strong opposition force in the new PLC (Palestinian Legislative Council) and push political and administrative reforms. The final results came as shock for Fatah and a surprise for Hamas – 74 seats for Hamas and 45 for Fatah. This does not take into account the four seats gained by independents close to Hamas.

The election results not only placed the burden of government on Hamas' shoulders, but also gave rise to important challenges. How would Hamas deal with the internal political situation? How should it respond to pressure from Israel and the international community? How could it secure donor support? Would armed resistance still be an option? Hamas' initial reactions were confused and contradictory. The international pressure that built up after the elections, however, helped Hamas to define relatively quickly an official position that reflected balance and pragmatism. This paper looks at some of the challenges that Hamas faces in the area of governance. With transparency and accountability placed high on its electoral platform, Hamas has now to come up with a political programme that translates these slogans into practice. The following lays out options, strategies and constraints for a Hamas-led government in strengthening Palestinian governance.

Hamas' Approach

Islam, Democracy and International Relations

In contrast to many other Islamist movements, Hamas has always adopted a moderate political and social interpretation of Islam. Hamas never promoted revolutionary ideals, and it never advocated or endorsed the overthrow of national governments, either in the region or in the West. Hamas believes that the concept of democracy is quite compatible with the Islamic notion of *ashshoura* ('consultation'). The only difference lies in the conceptual source: the social and political values guiding the *ash-shoura* process are derived from the *Qur'an* and the *Sunna*. In Hamas' view the nature of the framework for governance – caliphate, kingdom, republic – is secondary and to be decided by the Muslims. What is crucial is that laws and values be based on the *Qur'an*.

Hamas also believes that political change should be decided at the ballot box in free and fair elections; it opposes violent change and rejects the notion of coup d'etat. Hamas values the freedom of speech and the press and has never used force to impose the principles of Islam. On the contrary, Hamas opposes forcing social values upon society – such as the veiling of women, for instance – and relies on dialogue and education instead. It is in line with these values that Hamas advocates a strong and vibrant Palestinian civil society. Political diversity and the participation of non-governmental organisations (NGOs) in the political process will be necessary if Palestinian state-building efforts are to succeed.

Importantly, Hamas has the religious conviction that Islam calls for dialogue with other religions – be it Judaism, Christianity, or any other. Hamas has established lasting relations with the Christian community in the occupied Palestinian territory; it has fielded Christian candidates on its election lists and has won large electoral support in predominantly Christian neighbourhoods, villages and towns. It is important to understand that the confrontation between Hamas and Israel is political and not religious. Hamas fights Israelis, not because they are Jews or of a different ethnic identity, but because they occupy Palestinian land.

In the view of Hamas, the liberation of Palestinian land from Israeli occupation is the most urgent and important objective, taking priority over the contentious question of the 'Islamic state.' In other words, Hamas continues to see itself primarily as a liberation movement. Only when the liberation of the land is achieved, can the question of the political system be put on the table.

Which specific form the governance system may take will be left solely to the Palestinian people, and Hamas will unconditionally accept this choice irrespective of the outcome. Although it is true that Hamas perceives Islam as the best way of tackling the problems of the Palestinian nation, it also strongly believes in gradual, reformatory and 'locally-owned' processes. Hamas propagates and implements Islam through education, socio-political institution-building and academic work; *jihad* against the Israeli occupation is another important pillar of Islamic practice.

Hamas derives its ideology from the *ikhwan* – the Muslim Brotherhood. To this day, it officially follows the decisions and general policies of the *ikhwan* which its sees as the 'mother movement.' Having based its policies and activities on the principles of participation and inclusion, the Brotherhood has become part of the formal political system in most countries of the region. The Brotherhood's success as a political movement is based on its emphasis of grass-roots and community work and its strong involvement in social reform processes. Thereby the *ikhwan* has managed to mobilise large segments of the public; in fact, this is also how Hamas began its activity in the 1970s and 1980s. However, given that the Palestinians have remained under foreign occupation ever since, Hamas has adopted the military option. In contrast, the *ikhwan* organisations in neighbouring countries reject the use of violence against their governments.

Hamas pursues a strict policy of non-alignment and is interested in keeping its decision-making free from foreign influence. It does not side or align itself with any specific state in the region – be it Iran, Syria or any other Arab government. In fact, Hamas is very cautious not to repeat what it considers the strategic mistake of the PLO (Palestine Liberation Organisation); changing its ideology as a function of changes in its political alliances weakened the PLO and undermined its struggle against occupation.

110

Naturally, Hamas has normal and friendly relations with the *ikhwan* organisations in different Arab states, with which it shares its ideological and organisational origins. However, it categorically rejects interference in the affairs of any other state.

Concepts of Transparency and Accountability

Hamas' understanding of transparency and accountability does not essentially differ from those held in the West. For Hamas, transparency primarily means openness and free access to information. All public institutions, in particular the Executive, but also the Legislature and the Judiciary, shall provide the citizens with accurate information about their actions and not hide anything from the public.

Transparency in governance is a necessary precondition for accountability. For Hamas, accountability means that public institutions shall be answerable to the people and respond to their needs and concerns. This includes a fair, equitable public service, based on the rule of law, as well as mechanisms to hold institutions responsible if they fail to meet these conditions. In Hamas' view, the principle of accountability is comprehensive and applies to all governance and public institutions; it is the safeguard and antidote against corruption.[1]

Hamas derives these concepts from the *Qur'an*, which makes ample reference to the principles of transparency and accountability. Indeed, both concepts constitute a core message of Islam which applies to the political, social and individual realm:

> 'Allah does not call you to account for what is vain in your oaths, but He will call you to account for what your hearts have earned, and Allah is Forgiving, Forbearing.'[2]

> 'Whatever is in the heavens and whatever is on the earth is Allah's; and whether you manifest what is in your minds or hide it, Allah will call you to account according to it; then He will forgive whom He pleases and chastise whom He pleases, and Allah has power over all things.'[3]

In terms of governance, the principles of transparency and accountability are included in the concept of *ash-shoura:*

> 'And those who respond to their Lord and keep up prayer, and their rule is to take counsel among themselves, and who spend out of what We have given them.'[4]

Ash-shoura means that the Islamic ruler is required to learn the views of the people when running the affairs of the Muslims. The consultation process must ensure that his final decision is acceptable to the public. This system was applied by the Prophet Mohammad – peace and blessings be upon him – throughout his life on many occasions, as stated in the *Sunna*. In fact, Muslims who had experienced the conduct of the Prophet were so aware of accountability that there was strong protest when the regime of a later Caliph deviated from it.

Throughout Islamic history, the majority of Islamic scholars and jurists have opined in favour of transparency and accountability. Sheikh Yussef Qaradawi, a contemporary scholar, Head of the European Council on Fatwa and Research and an influential preacher, has also contributed to the evolution of Islamic precepts on reform, good governance and anticorruption.

In this regard, Hamas' conceptions also differ from the Shiite notion of *wilayat al-faqih*, which states that the ruler is imposed by God and is therefore infallible. In contrast, in Sunni Islam the ruler is selected by the people. As a human being, he is capable of making mistakes.

The Need for Transparency and Accountability

Enhancing transparency and accountability in governance will be the only way out of the current political and socio-economic crisis in Palestine. It cannot be emphasised enough that transparency and accountability must extend to all levels of governance. Hamas believes that political, economic and social processes cannot be separated and thus advocates a comprehensive reform approach.

The importance of implementing transparency and accountability rests on several factors. First of all, good and clean governance will save the Palestinians political energy, funds and time; it will also enable Palestinians to develop their administrative and managerial skills. Secondly, transparency and accountability are a key precondition for improving the relations between the citizens and the PNA (Palestinian National Authority). Effective and efficient administrative procedures and constant contact between the government and the people will result in more responsive governance and help enhance mutual trust and respect. In turn, good and trustful relations between the government and the people are a prerequisite for political and social stability and the democratic transition of power. A third and related point is that effective and accountable institutions, particularly in relation to justice and security, will discourage people from taking the law into their own hands. Fourthly, transparent and accountable governance will renew the trust of the donor community; at the same time, it will improve the prospects of economic development by encouraging investment.

Although Hamas does not expect progress on the peace track any time soon, all of the above will put the Palestinians and their government in a better position to realise their demands vis-à-vis Israel. In fact, Hamas feels that it can only begin to tackle the hard political issues in relation to Israel once the internal reform process is well under way. In this regard, Hamas desperately needs the support of the citizens; as long as Palestinians do not enjoy a minimum of physical security, economic stability and good governance, they will not support Hamas on the political front.

Finally, the experience of governance will also provide an opportunity for Hamas itself to become more open. Government members committed to strengthening transparency and accountability in their institutions will have to apply the same principles inside the movement. Although some sectors of Hamas will remain secret for security reasons, the movement's general structure, internal organisation and personnel structure will become much more transparent to the public, a process that has already started.

Challenges for Hamas in Government

Defining Policy Priorities

The new Palestinian government faces many difficult challenges. These range from the relations with Israel to the domestic situation in political, security and economic terms. Palestinian living conditions have deteriorated so dramatically over recent years that Hamas will need to focus its attention primarily on the domestic scene.

As a matter of priority, reforms are needed in three areas. Firstly, the Hamas government will have to take tangible steps to end the state of lawlessness in the occupied Palestinian territory. It will have to impose law and order on the streets and secure the physical safety of the Palestinian citizens. Secondly, Hamas will enhance the performance of the public administration and undertake serious steps to tackle institutional corruption. Thirdly, on the economic front Hamas will have to revive the economy in order to create new job opportunities, reduce unemployment and improve the living conditions of Palestinians. The previous government's failure to achieve tangible progress in any of these areas has propelled Hamas to electoral victory. Consequently, public support for and trust in the new government will depend on Hamas' ability to impose law and order, curb corruption and deliver better services and more jobs.

Restoring Trust in Institutions

A sharp decline in Palestinian living conditions and, since 2000, progressive institutional disintegration in the PNA, have undermined public trust and widened the gap between citizens and public institutions. Palestinians simply feel that they do not own the public institutions. Endemic corruption and the misuse of funds have aggravated this perception. Only recently, investigations by the Palestinian Attorney-General have brought to light the magnitude of the problem and the degree of involvement of Palestine's political and economic elite.

Hamas is committed to strengthening public institutions in order to develop Palestinian society and lay the foundations of a future state. Good governance of institutions requires the rule of law and qualified individuals capable of managing them. With the establishing of the PNA and the PLC, Palestinians have already made progress towards building an institutional framework for governance. Now, the time has come to free both the PNA and the PLC from the deficiencies that have crippled their performance in the past and to reform them to enhance their effectiveness. Yet, institutional reform alone will not be enough. Reform and change must also apply to civil society, the Palestinian non-governmental organisations, and the individual. Only a comprehensive reform process offers the Palestinians an opportunity to lift themselves out of the misery in which years of economic deterioration and distorted social values have left them.

Managing Relations with Fatah

Fatah's domination of the PNA presents a heavy political and institutional legacy for the Hamas government. Over the past 12 years, relations between both movements have been strained. The tensions have been kept alive because Fatah claimed a monopoly in representing the Palestinian national movement and showed unwillingness to compromise. Fatah's long unrivalled control of the PNA has resulted in an inflated public sector with more than 160,000 employees, massive structural inefficiencies, partisan recruitment and a lack of accountability. Fatah is also responsible for the PNA's massive debt burden (around $600 million) and the huge public deficit (around $1 billion).

Importantly, Fatah also controls the PNA security forces; it is therefore unclear whether the security sector will cooperate with a Hamas government and, if it does, to what extent.

The situation is exacerbated by the fact that in the run-up to the January elections Fatah recruited thousands of party affiliates into ministries, public administration and the security sector. Fatah also deliberately put party affiliates in key positions in the PLC and the PNA Bureau for Administrative and Financial Control and the General Personnel Council, so as to hamper any reforms that Hamas might undertake. Hamas therefore expects resistance and foot-dragging from the Fatah-dominated bureaucracy in the course of its reform programme. In the worst case, tensions between Hamas and Fatah might even lead to a stalemate between the government and the President's Office, with both institutions blocking each other.

Overcoming External Constraints

Several external factors will make it difficult for Hamas to push ahead with the internal reform process. Israel and important international actors were putting the Palestinians under severe diplomatic and economic pressure weeks before a Hamas government was even formed. Israel is also preventing the transfer to the PNA of collected tax and customs revenues, which are the legal property of the PNA. Furthermore, Israel has added to the economic hardship by stepping up its military activities in the occupied territory and by denying Palestinian workers entry into Israel.

Such action could lead to increased instability and chaos in the occupied territories, especially if it were combined with a massive reduction in international aid which would force the PNA to suspend salary payments to public sector employees. International actors rightly fear that a collapse of the PNA and the ensuing chaos might endanger their interests in the region. However, they may underestimate the speed with which such a situation could unfold if nothing were done to prevent it from happening.

Some donors proposed that international aid be channelled through international organisations and NGOs. Hamas opposes this idea, because it attaches importance to institutional development. The setting up of an institutional framework parallel to the existing PNA institutions, Hamas fears, would undermine the state-building process.

Managing relations with Arab states poses no less of a challenge. The Hamas government clearly needs 'Arab legitimacy' and support from regional actors. However, some Arab governments might side with the US Administration and endorse the American policy of politically isolating Hamas. Without doubt there will be a strong need for Hamas to boost relations with the Arab and wider Islamic world and receive their political and financial support, especially if Western states continue to pressure the Palestinian government. The visits of its delegations to Egypt, Iran, Qatar, Syria and Turkey in February and March 2006 gave hope to Hamas that it would obtain support from these states, and be able to count on a political and financial safety net.

Towards a Hamas Reform Strategy

Limitations

Any realistic strategy for internal reform needs to be concerned with its limitations. The biggest obstacles for Hamas are related to the ongoing Israeli occupation. The annexation of occupied territory; fragmentation of the West Bank by settlements, infrastructure projects, and road-blocks; and the siege of Gaza have resulted in the physical separation of Gaza, the West Bank and East Jerusalem, which today impedes effective contact, communication and cooperation amongst Palestinians. Strong international pressure, attempts at political isolation, domestic political constraints, and socio-economic conditions constitute additional obstacles. Hamas is also under serious time pressure; on the one hand, a four-year term is too short for implementing a comprehensive reform programme, and on the other, Palestinians are impatient for quick and tangible results.

The combination of all these factors constrains the available options for Hamas. The new government will thus have to define priorities and balance stakeholder interests. It has a chance to make significant progress if it opts for a carefully calibrated strategy combining three elements: (1) securing the truce; (2) managing relations with Fatah through political accommodation; and (3) improving governance by making institutions more transparent and accountable.

Securing the Truce

Hamas and the new government are determined to make a contribution to calming the situation by reiterating their commitment to truce made in March 2005. Hamas is prepared to start implementing it unilaterally, even at a time when it is unclear whether such a commitment will be reciprocated by Israel. Hamas sees a clear danger that any Israeli military escalation will force Palestinians to retaliate. This could draw the region into a new cycle of violence. The Hamas government therefore seeks to reach an understanding with the different factions of the Palestinian resistance, convincing them to work in one cohesive framework. This would also have to include an understanding on how militant factions would react in specific situations.

Managing the Opposition

A 'grand coalition' with Fatah would have made the tasks of the new government significantly easier. Fatah, inexperienced at sharing power and unwilling to make such a compromise, has opted to stay out of the government. This leaves Hamas to govern on its own. Nevertheless, Hamas has no other choice but to develop, over time, a solid relationship with Fatah, as the movement still enjoys large popular support.

Hamas therefore strives to maintain close relations with Fatah and consult with the opposition on all policy issues. Hamas will make every effort in order to connect to those in Fatah who are interested in cooperation between the two movements. Under no circumstances will Hamas risk violent clashes with Fatah for these would have the potential to get rapidly out of control.

Hamas and Fatah need to formulate in writing a clear set of agreed principles that guide their future relations and their approach to internal and external challenges. The earlier such guiding principles are formulated, the better. Hamas is also considering the establishment of a special consultation committee with representatives of both parties. The Palestinian Legislative Council, which has now become much more diverse, also calls for a careful management of relations. Hamas is prepared to offer the opposition the chairs of various important PLC committees, such as the Committee for Oversight of Human Rights and Public Freedoms.

Hamas is also keen to maintain close relations with the President of the Palestinian National Authority and is prepared to show a high degree of flexibility. This means that Hamas has no objection to Mahmoud Abbas proceeding on the path of negotiations with Israel. Hamas will seek to avoid any confrontation with the President's Office and refrain from putting obstacles in the President's way. Mahmoud Abbas may play an even more important role in future Palestinian politics and serve as a bridge between Hamas and Fatah.

Improving Governance

While more transparency and accountability are needed in all sectors, the many constraints force the government to identify clear policy priorities. Hamas plans to focus on three objectives to improve transparency and accountability:

(1) restoring the functioning of the Palestinian judiciary; (2) strengthening legislative and executive oversight mechanisms; and (3) enhancing the performance of the government. The guiding principle thereby will be to establish a clear separation of powers between the Executive, the PLC and the Judiciary.

Even in these defined areas, progress will not be easy and will require time; resistance from employees or political blockades might very well hamper the implementation of specific reform measures, as might the lack of funding. The Hamas government will therefore proceed carefully and gradually; for the time being, it will desist from radical measures such as systematic purges of corrupt officials or large-scale downsizing of public institutions. Hamas will also need some time to define timelines and indicators for the reform process and determine funding requirements.

Activating the Judiciary: The PNA Judiciary has suffered from years of neglect. Establishing security in the occupied territories requires fair, effective and efficient judicial procedures, which will prevent the citizens from taking the law into their own hands or seeking judicial support from traditional mechanisms of adjudication. The Hamas government will work to strengthen the capacity of courts and judges and to reduce the current backlog of cases. It is also considering the introduction of a public complaints mechanism to the Judiciary.

Hamas will moreover strengthen the institution of the Attorney-General which has long underperformed due to the lack of political support from the government. The Attorney-General needs to be given more extended powers, more support staff and funding in order to become the institutional 'referee' who can guarantee improved accountability.

Strengthening Legislative Oversight: Hamas will put special emphasis on boosting the oversight capacity of the PLC. The PLC Committees have wide oversight powers which have not been properly used in the past. The Hamas majority in parliament will work to activate these committees and optimise their working procedures. Special attention will be devoted to strengthening the capacities of the Interior and Security Committee, which will be the watchdog over the security sector and cooperate closely with the Attorney-General. Hamas is furthermore in favour of creating an effective parliamentary complaints mechanism for citizens.

Hamas will also work to establish a cohesive legal framework for transparency and accountability. It will review the existing legislation, implement effective laws as soon as possible, and devise new laws where necessary. A special focus will be on the amendment of the legislation dealing with corruption. Some draft legislation such as the Political Party Law requires more discussion.

Enhancing Executive Accountability: The new government aims to establish sound accountability and oversight mechanisms in the Executive. Hamas plans to set up a complaints department in each ministry which will work closely with the PLC and the Attorney-General. Each cabinet member will give due importance to the enhancement of transparency in his ministry. The government will furthermore activate and strengthen the Bureau of Financial and Administrative Control, the PNA's auditing department, and ensure its smooth cooperation with all other oversight bodies.

Streamlining Governmental Institutions: There is a dire need to streamline governmental institutions and increase the productivity of ministerial employees; some 20 per cent of the workforce on the governmental payroll do not show up for work. Overstaffing puts a heavy burden on the budget and calls for systematic downsizing of the public administration. Hamas believes that some ministries are needless and only cause deficits in the budget; they could be easily transformed into government departments or merged with other ministries.

For the time being, however, Hamas will not systematically lay off personnel, given the dire economic situation in the occupied territories. Instead, it will keep the existing ministries and departments and enhance its administrative capacities through pushing employees to work. High on the list in this regard are the Ministries of Health, Economy, Social Security and Local Governance. The government might also dismiss some of the recently recruited employees in various ministries, such as Foreign Affairs and Information.

Improving the Performance of Security Organisations: The PNA security organisations have underperformed in the past. They are responsible for the security chaos in the occupied territories. The PLC has never been able to hold to account the security branches, which hitherto have been controlled by Fatah. However, Hamas wants to make sure that the security forces belong to all Palestinians. Their mission must be to protect the Palestinians from crime and internal disorder, as well as from Israeli aggression.

The Hamas government has authority over most security organisations, only some are under the authority of the President. Hamas will therefore work to establish cooperative relations between the government and the President's Office and coordinate closely with the President all issues related to security sector governance. The government will furthermore initiate a trust-building dialogue with the security commanders. It will also establish effective parliamentary oversight over the security sector through the PLC committees.

Enhancing Planning and Research Capacities: The Hamas government will systematically use the work of research and academic institutions to improve the planning capacities of the Executive. 'Lessons learned' should be documented and analysed in order to avoid the mistakes made by the past government. Systematic efforts will be made to study public opinion. Great importance will be given to the development of clear indicators for the government to measure reform progress. Such indicators could include economic growth rates, employment rates, access to courts, and public perceptions of security.

Acquiring Professional Expertise: Hamas will recruit qualified, experienced and honest individuals into the PNA institutions, particularly in managerial positions. This will also help to reduce the risk of corruption. Hamas has already made a step in this direction by putting capable and respected persons on its elections list, but further concerted efforts will have to be undertaken to recruit renowned experts in fields such as economics, health and education.

Strengthening Communication with Citizens: The Hamas government will seek to develop the trust of citizens by improving communication. Hamas needs to make every effort to avoid the errors of the previous government, which systematically neglected the needs and concerns of the public and eventually lost the people's trust. Hamas will have to develop a sound communications strategy, as well as the necessary mechanisms and infrastructure. On a related issue, the new government should also embark on a public awareness campaign in order to enhance the citizens' understanding of law and order; notions of order, discipline and the rule of law should be included in school and university curricula.

Conclusion

The future success of Hamas in government hinges to a great extent on its ability to improve Palestinian governance and enhance transparency and accountability. A whole range of domestic and international factors make this a difficult task. In order to address this challenge, Hamas hopes for the continuing support of the international community, especially the European Union and the United States. The withdrawal of financial aid would almost certainly lead to the collapse of Palestinian institutions, chaos and instability. Hamas also calls upon the West to devise a clear political vision of how to solve the conflict between the Palestinians and Israelis, based on the recognition of Palestinian rights and providing a modus vivendi for both parties. Hamas is aware of the difficulty of such a step but sees it as crucial for maintaining stability in the region.

For its part, Hamas is ready to deal with the West and display an utmost degree of openness and transparency in governance, so that donors will be able to see in detail where their aid has gone. And although Hamas feels that the demands of the West are politically motivated, it has displayed much flexibility over the last months. It has offered a long-term truce and has modified its rejectionist stance towards the agreements concluded between Palestinians and Israelis. However, accepting all three Western demands, including the recognition of Israel, will not be easy.

Yet, in the face of all these obstacles, Hamas is strongly committed to its internal reform strategy and will work strenuously for its implementation. Hamas' success in doing so will open a new phase for the Palestinian people and give them hope to surpass the crises of the past. Successful governance by Hamas will also nurture political change in the Arab World and encourage other Islamic movements to follow the model of peaceful and democratic transition of power. Thereby it will also help bridge the widening gap between the Arab and Islamic world and the West.

Notes

1   In Hamas' understanding, 'corruption' has a political, economic and moral dimension. Politically, it is the refusal to use authority in the service of the public; economically, it refers to the misuse of public funds; and morally to the abuse of trust.
2   Sura *al-baqara*, verse 2.225.
3   Ibid., verse 2.284.
4   Sura *ash-shoura*, verse 42.38.

Entry-Points to Palestinian Security Sector Reform

Roland Friedrich and Arnold Luethold

Political life in the Palestinian Territories is undergoing a painful transition from external rule to some form of statehood. At present, the outcome of this process seems difficult to picture. While various Palestinian groups hold different views as to where this transition process should eventually lead, most of them seem to agree that a well-functioning security sector will be a prerequisite for any form of political success. Security sector reform is thus not an end in itself, but a necessary step in the political development towards Palestinian self-determination.

As the authors in this volume have illustrated, security sector reform is a complex political and social process rather than a technical endeavour. Reorganising and restructuring security forces alone would not produce capable security and justice providers for Palestinian society. Nor would training and equipment be able to achieve it. Legitimate, effective security and justice organisations emerge from a broad range of inter-related and mutually reinforcing efforts. They would be unable to perform well without technical skills or proper equipment, but their real strength stems from public trust and support. This, in turn, requires an efficient political management.

In this book, Palestinian authors describe why reform efforts by the Palestinian security sector itself and by international supporters have failed to gain the trust and confidence of the Palestinian people. They offer their views on how the sector needs to change to enhance its image and provide better service to the people. Many of their recommendations point to the need for broader consultation and participation and for greater respect for legal and institutional processes. The proposed reform agenda is very broad. It includes constitutional, legal, institutional, cultural, political, organisational and structural change and involves many different stakeholder groups.

For reform to get under way, it is important to find an entry-point. The Palestinian security sector provides in fact not one, but many different starting points for system-wide reform. However, a successful reform programme will need to address them all at some point, because they are all interlinked and constitute only different aspects of the same problem. In addition, Palestinian SSR will have to deal with several other issues, which are important to success, but inappropriate as a launching pad for reform, as for example the disarmament of non-statutory armed groups.

In the interest of stimulating a rethinking of security sector reform in the Palestinian context, the following highlights some of the entry points that have come forward from the contributions in this book.

Creating an Enabling Environment

The Palestinian writers who have contributed to this volume perceive Israeli occupation as a major impediment to Palestinian SSR. Yet, they refrain from putting all the blame for the stagnant reforms on the Occupying Power and analyse instead the Palestinian share of responsibility for weak security sector governance. They all concede that Palestinians can and must improve governance of their security sector, despite the occupation. However, they also demonstrate the difficulties for any Palestinian government to advance reforms, as long as it has only very limited control of key parameters.

The separation between Gaza and the West Bank and severe travel restrictions prevent Palestinian legislators, security personnel and technical experts from moving about freely. Thus, meetings and cooperation have become extremely difficult and time-consuming, if not impossible. Further obstacles to mobility and control stem from the progressive fragmentation of territory, which comes with the construction and expansion of settlements, the erection of the separation barrier, and the isolation of East Jerusalem from the West Bank. The financial and diplomatic boycotts of the Hamas government, the widespread arrests of elected representatives and the renewed destruction of Palestinian security infrastructure in 2006, have incapacitated Palestinian institutions. Palestinians believe that external actors have paid too much attention to Israeli and not enough to Palestinian security interests. In the Palestinian perception, all this has undermined trust in their political leadership, the international community and hopes for a just and peaceful settlement.

Because sponsors of reform need political capital on which they can rely, the environment ought to be supportive of reform. Unless Israel, the US, the EU and Russia accept the integration of Palestinian security concerns into the equation and adjust their policies accordingly, Palestinian reformers will have a difficult stance, and SSR will see only modest progress, if any.

An ineffective and poorly-governed Palestinian security sector not only fails to deliver security and justice to Palestinians, but is also unable to deliver what the international community might expect from it in terms of security guarantees for Israel. Some in the international community may have been aware that Hamas would have never been able to meet the conditions for obtaining international acceptance and recognition, because of the poor governance it inherited, particularly in the security sector. By making a precondition for governing what is in fact the outcome of successful governing, the international community is guilty of either blundering or of acting cynically. The political blockage that has resulted from this international attitude constitutes the most important obstacle to reform. Thus, investing in a political environment conducive to reform opens the way to comprehensive security sector reform and better security for all.

Developing the Normative-Legal Framework

Asem Khalil has demonstrated that Palestinians lack a cohesive legal framework for security sector governance, despite past efforts to regulate the security sector. In his analysis, Khalil pointed at *legal inconsistencies* between the *Basic Security Draft Law* and other security legislation and *normative inconsistencies* between legal norms and political norms. Several legal provisions, for example, are not in line with the civil-democratic standards to which Palestinian society claims to adhere. Khalil attributes this incongruence to the fact that security commanders had too much control over the drafting process and could directly interfere with it.

The review of the normative and legal framework remains thus an important entry-point to Palestinian SSR. As Khalil proposed, the main purpose of a legal review and reform process would be to base security sector governance on a sound *Basic Security Law* and to make sure that the various norms are compatible with each other. For enhanced oversight, the PLC, the Judiciary and the Bureau of Financial and Administrative Control would need improved legislation. In order to overcome some of the weaknesses described, the drafting process itself would require attention; it would notably have to be designed in a way that prevents interest groups from gaining control over it.

Strengthening Executive Oversight

The authors in this volume have illustrated how the domination of the National Authority and its institutions by one political faction prevented the emergence of effective control mechanisms and crippled many reform initiatives. Fatah's refusal to relinquish control of the bureaucracy and the security organisations after its electoral defeat has aggravated and escalated the situation; it has led to institutional paralysis and to an unprecedented level of political polarisation. Some donor countries have also contributed to this development by encouraging confrontation and assisting selected groups within Fatah to force regimechange. This moved security sector governance further away from institutional process and made it again dependent on a few individuals.

From the viewpoint of all contributors to this book, such a policy is shortsighted, externally driven, and not sustainable. If building peace and stability remains the overall objective, a more promising strategy for achieving it would be to promote political and institutional development; Hamas and Fatah would need to be encouraged to accept compromise and share power, based on fair process; they would need to cooperate in order to develop some sort of consensus. Without institutional support, it will be impossible to reconcile the competing interests of different stakeholder groups and to guarantee the rule of law. Decision-makers who get their advice from individuals rather than from institutions risk making poor decisions, because they often fail to understand properly the benefits and costs associated with their choices. In strategic decision-making, over-reliance on individuals tends to result in frequent overturning of strategic decisions, undercutting development and producing additional costs for society.

As another possible starting point for security sector reform, the writers in this book suggest that Palestinians review their institutional setup and make changes, where necessary. Palestinians must reach a conclusion as to whether the executive institutions they have can be changed to better fit their needs or have to be replaced and/or supplemented by new ones. The authors in this book have expressed a strong demand for a clearer delineation of responsibilities, mainly between the President, the Prime Minister and the Minister of the Interior, and for enhanced coordination among Palestinian political actors. Whether the National Security Council (NSC) shall assume overall coordination in security affairs, or what its composition should be, or how much discretionary power the Prime Minister should have, are important decisions, which require political consensus and must therefore be part of an inclusive political process.

Strengthening Parliamentary Oversight

For much of the last ten years, the Palestinian Legislative Council has largely neglected its oversight role in the security sector. If it has been slightly more assertive, following the change in the Palestinian presidency, its overall performance has not been convincing. As Majed Arouri and Mamoun Attili have shown, security sector oversight limited itself to sporadic inquiries and hearings of officials; in many cases, the Executive refused to share information with the Council and thereby impeded it from assuming its oversight function. The lack of cooperation was particularly evident in the disregard of budgetary legislation: draft budgets were not only regularly incomplete, but also reached parliament with great delays. Thus the PLC knew close to nothing about the revenues and expenses of the different security organisations. Arouri and Attili attribute the reasons for the PLC's poor performance in part to the monolithic power structure of the Palestinian Authority and in part to a lack of parliamentary experience.

Advocating stronger parliamentary oversight at a time when the Palestinian legislature is isolated and actively prevented from carrying out its work may appear anachronistic. Yet, for moving towards good governance in the security sector, the authors see no alternative to respecting and engaging institutions that are representative of the Palestinian electoral will. International political pressure may succeed in temporarily delaying, but not in preventing parliament from becoming a more assertive actor in the security sector. Developing parliamentary oversight capacity thus remains a priority for comprehensive security sector reform. On the Palestinian side, some of the concrete development measures would have to include:

- empowering the relevant PLC committees (Interior and Security, Human Rights and Public Freedoms, Budget and Financial Affairs, and Legal Affairs);
- improving parliamentary access to information;
- developing parliamentary expertise in matters related to oversight, with a strong focus on budgetary oversight;
- fostering a culture of cooperation, both between the factions in the PLC and between the PLC and the Executive.

Strengthening Judicial Oversight

In many regards, the Judiciary remains the weakest and institutionally least developed sector of the PNA. The absence of a cohesive legal framework, the proliferation of judicial institutions with overlapping mandates, and the lack of funding and trained staff are, as Maen Id'ais has pointed out, only some of the major problems that plague the Palestinian justice system. As with the PNA security organisations, the judicial institutions also have to struggle with political interference and the lack of political will to conduct thorough reforms.

All these factors hamper court administration. They lead to the accumulation of cases and prevent the implementation of court decisions. The weakness of the Judiciary has encouraged the resurgence of Palestinian customary tribal law and other informal mechanisms of conflict resolution. This in itself is not necessarily a negative development, because it helps regulate social conflicts, but, in the longer term, the rise of tribal law, at the expense of the official Judiciary, undermines the Palestinian state-building process.

Id'ais has drawn attention to the difficulty of establishing rule of law in a context where judicial oversight over security organisations is weak and where cooperation between the Judiciary and the security organisations is almost nonexistent. As a way forward and as another entry-point to security sector reform, he called for a clearer definition of responsibilities and better coordination between the Judiciary and the security forces, in particular between the Public Prosecution and the *Civil Police*. Other priority issues would involve the resolution of the conflict between the Ministry of Justice and the High Judicial Council and the reform of the military court system.

Developing Public Oversight

Developing civil society involvement in security sector governance is one of the biggest challenges to Palestinian SSR. Despite strong and widespread popular support for comprehensive security sector reform, the Palestinian public has little information on on-going SSR activities and hardly plays any role in them.

Security sector governance remains for many officials a sensitive topic, and reluctance to discuss it in public is still widespread. Even the Palestinian media partly shy away from covering issues linked to security sector governance. Until now, the chief impediments to media coverage have been restricted access to information and lack of expertise in analysing the limited information available.

Though Majed Arouri and Mamoun Attili have emphasised the efforts of Palestinian human rights organisations in strengthening accountability of security officials, they also have drawn attention to the limitations of civil society in a governance system that lacks effective legislative and judicial oversight and operates in a closed manner. As part of a comprehensive reform process, they nevertheless make the case for greater public oversight and propose that NGOs, think tanks, research institutions and the media acquire the requisite expertise for helping develop an informed debate. Public interest is stimulated when citizens feel that the authorities deal with their grievances and requests. The establishing of the Palestinian Independent Commission for Citizens' Rights (PICCR), as a national ombudsman, has been a step in the right direction. For turning it into an effective tool of public oversight, the PNA would have to provide it with a clear legal basis.

Determining Strategic Direction of SSR

Several comments in the preceding chapters highlight the lack of strategic direction in the Palestinians' security decision-making. Palestinians have no shared understanding of what 'security' means to them; the positions of Hamas and Fatah point in opposite directions. In the absence of a consensus, the parties are also unable to develop a compromise and to agree on the division of labour amongst the various components of the security sector or on an overall security policy.

Past attempts to streamline security thinking have failed, mostly because they lacked inclusiveness. A good example for this is the White Paper for Palestinian Security, which a small group of PNA officials tried to develop in 2005 with the support of the United States and other donors. The White Paper was meant to provide a blueprint for the division of labour within the security sector and to outline principles for depoliticising and professionalising Palestinian forces. The attempt eventually failed, because the process was elite-driven and dominated by a small group of Executive officials; it had failed to systematically involve representatives from parliament and civil society; and it had tried to codify a vision of Palestinian security that did not address the needs and concerns of the wider public.

Developing a nationally-owned security policy is one of the most urgent and most difficult challenges of Palestinian SSR. It is a complicated and lengthy political process in which the participation and input of all important Palestinian stakeholder groups is needed. A national security policy which is legitimate and accepted by the public would provide a framework for assessing options of reform and help ensure that the overall direction of reform advances long-term public rather than short-term private interests. It would also help mobilise the public support and patience needed for implementing a policy which may take investment and time before yielding its benefits. Broad-based consultation, consensus and compromise are essential preconditions for sustainable Palestinian SSR and therefore link success of reform to some sort of power-sharing agreement between the major Palestinian actors.

A national security policy would ideally be developed through an inclusive process that involves all stakeholders in Palestinian security sector governance, especially the main political factions and civil society. As the White Paper process has demonstrated, exclusive and non-participatory approaches in this regard are bound to fail.

Managing Donor Assistance to SSR

Few observers doubt that Palestinian SSR can succeed without external support. However, Palestinians regard the massive outside involvement in the process as a double-edged sword. On the one hand, donor support is indispensable for creating an effective, efficient and democratically accountable PNA security sector. On the other hand, there is a clear tension between Palestinian needs and concerns and the objectives of external actors.

The notion of Palestinian statehood and full sovereignty is eventually incompatible with the US and Israeli vision of limited policing authority for the PNA. Ahmad Hussein has drawn attention to the perils of uncoordinated and politically-motivated donor involvement in SSR. In the best case, such an approach results in the waste of resources, expertise and political capital. In the worst case, it undermines the whole SSR process and with it the process of peace- and state-building.

For example, the US initiative to train and equip the *Presidential Guard* and the *National Security Forces* to counter the new Hamas government has had four important drawbacks: (1) It established a new PNA security organisation outside governmental and parliamentary control; this runs counter to what security sector reform seeks to achieve, namely a democratically-accountable and legitimate security sector. (2) It heightened tensions between Hamas and Fatah; the bloody clashes of 2007, which ended in Hamas' seizure of control in the Gaza Strip, were a direct consequence of this policy. (3) The disregard for proper institutional process, mainly in terms of resource allocation, strategic and operational control, and accountability procedures, resulted in the progressive dissolution of institutions and subsequently accelerated the breakdown of central control and fragmentation of political power. (4) Ultimately it also undermined the credibility of donor involvement. According to a DCAF poll, 84 per cent of Palestinians distrusted the advice and assistance given by the US and Canada in security sector governance; and 69 per cent distrusted European advice and assistance in this regard.[1]

From a development perspective, SSR built on a hardcore security notion that neglects the importance of political development for achieving long-term stability is part of the problem, not of the solution.

Thus, establishing mechanisms for managing and coordinating donor assistance can become an important starting point for security sector reform.

Close political scrutiny of donor programmes ought to ensure that assistance responds to identified needs, is compatible with long-term development objectives and benefits the society, not individuals or a particular group. On the receiving side, Palestinians need to be concerned with establishing proper oversight mechanisms – combining security and development expertise – which monitor donor activities and report on them. On the donor side, tighter control mechanisms over military, police and intelligence experts need to make sure that the design of SSR programmes abides by the criteria formulated by donor countries and thus seeks

(1) to improve security and justice for local communities;
(2) to strengthen governance and oversight over security organisations;
(3) to enhance local ownership;
(4) to increase the sustainability of justice and security service delivery through improved management of human and financial capital.[2]

Managing the Costs

Several chapters highlighted the fact that PNA security organisations are overstaffed and constitute a financial burden for Palestinian society. Out of the 85,000 security employees on the government payroll, some 25,000 to 35,000 do not report to work. However, even if the effective number did not exceed 50,000, this would still result in a police-to-population ration of 1:80, one of the highest in the world.

The security share of the public wage bill has grown by 80 per cent between 1999 and 2004. This figure does not even include the pension costs for security personnel that the PNA is obliged to pay.[3] With a projected annual budget deficit of some $900 million in 2006[4], Palestinians simply cannot afford the security organisations they have and will have to reduce them. Yet, amongst all reform measures, reducing is the least popular, because it would deprive a large number of families of much-needed income. Nevertheless, several authors call for improved financial management and better-controlled budgetary processes for security organisations.

Restructuring Security Organisations

Several authors emphasised that the PNA security organisations need structural transformation. Merging the existing security forces into three main organisations, Ahmad Hussein argues in his chapter, would help counter the proliferation of security organisations outside the existing framework and should therefore become a priority. He and others in this book demanded a clearer delineation of tasks for the *Internal Security Forces* and a better separation of law enforcement from intelligence activities. Further suggestions for organisational improvements aimed at establishing a unified command and control centre, developing interoperability amongst the Palestinian forces, and at upgrading planning and budgeting capabilities.

Conclusion

Nowhere else in the Arab region does security sector reform attract more passion than in the Palestinian Territories. Palestinian factions quarrel about the distribution of power, the role of law and institutions, the future direction of the society, the control of assets and the influence of foreign powers. All this is a rather healthy sign in a process of state formation. That Palestinians attach so much interest to security sector reform may also be seen as an indication that they understand what is at stake for them.

Rather than looking at this process as a threat, regional and international actors need to become more open to the many opportunities it holds. A fresh international approach to security sector reform could help realise some of them. Investing in long-term institutional development with functioning check-and-balance systems promises real dividends in terms of peace and stability, while short-term objectives delay solutions to problems and in the longer term increase the political risks.

As the contributions to this volume have shown, Palestinians from all factions have quite concrete ideas as to how their institutions should change. They might just need to be offered an opportunity to work together.

Notes

1   Roland Friedrich, Arnold Luethold, Luigi de Martino, *Government Change and Security Sector Governance: Palestinian Public Perceptions, Summary Report*, 3 August 2007, (Geneva: DCAF-IUED), pp. 25-26. Available at: http://www.dcaf.ch/mena/Palestine_Sec_ Perceptions.pdf.

2   See OECD, The OECD DAC Handbook on Security System Reform (SSR), 2007, p. 63

3   The Law of Insurance and Pensions for Palestinian Security Forces No. 16 of 2004 provides retirees a pension worth over 100 per cent of the final salary. As there are no security pension assets, and nearly all those personnel covered by the law are eligible for retirement upon the law's full implementation, all expenditures for this system will need to be met from PNA revenues, as opposed to any accumulated assets in a fund. The World Bank assesses the annual implementation costs at some \$40 million. Ibid., p. 49. World Bank, *The Palestinian Economy and the Prospects for its Recovery. Economic Monitoring Report to the Ad-Hoc Liaison Committee*, December 2005, pp. 8, 17.

Appendices

Appendix A

PNA Security Organisations

The personnel figures below reflect the number of PNA security personnel on the payroll as of September 2005. Massive recruitment into the PNA branches in Gaza, the incorporation of members of the *Al-Aqsa Brigades* and the creation of the *Executive Force* have brought the number of security personnel up to circa 85,000 (West Bank: 30,000; Gaza: 55,000) in May 2007, but no reliable data are available regarding the distribution of the newly-recruited personnel. Estimates of the current strength of *Preventive Security*, *General Intelligence*, *Executive Force*, *Presidential Guard* and the *National Security Forces* in total are included below. All figures below are based on open source information.

Even though they have been updated and consolidated in May 2007, they still constitute estimates and their accuracy may remain limited.

Internal Security Forces

The *Internal Security Forces* comprise the *Civil Police*, the *Preventive Security* and the *Civil Defence*. In 2002, these organisations were placed under the Ministry of the Interior. The Director-General for Internal Security commands the *Internal Security Forces*.

Civil Police

The *Civil Police* is the PNA's main law enforcement apparatus and handles ordinary police functions such as combating crime and upholding public order; it is also in charge of the PNA prisons. The *Civil Police* has various sub-branches such as the Criminal Investigations Department, the Anti-Drug-Department, the Public Order Forces, the Border Police, the Traffic Police, and the Women's Police. The *Civil Police* also has a rapid response unit, the Emergency Response Department. The organisation employs some 18,500 policemen, of whom about 12,000 are deployed in Gaza (including 3,100 Public Order Forces) and some 6,000 in the West Bank (including 1,000 Public Order Forces). The *Civil Police* wear dark blue uniforms, except for the Public Order Forces, which wear blue-black-white camouflage fatigues.

Preventive Security

The *Preventive Security*, an internal intelligence organisation, had in 2007 an estimated strength of 8,000 agents, 3,500 in the West Bank and 4,500 in Gaza. It has long been one the most powerful PNA intelligence organisations. Its main task, the protection of the *Oslo* peace process against internal opposition, involved action against Islamist factions and armed groups. In 2005 the Palestinian leadership announced the dismantling of the organisation's 'Security and Protection Department', the so-called 'Death Squad', which had been established in the late 1990s against activists of Hamas and Islamic Jihad. In practice, however, it has remained in place. To the *Preventive Security* belongs a well-equipped paramilitary unit in light green dress.

Civil Defence

The *Civil Defence* consists of the emergency and rescue services and the fire departments and has an approximate strength of 950.

National Security Forces

The *National Security Forces* are often described as the PNA's 'proto-army'. The *National Security Forces* are set to merge various organisations with military functions under a unified military command, including the actual *National Security Forces*, the *Naval Police*, the *Military Intelligence*, the *Military Liaison*, and possibly the *Presidential Security/Force 17*. No precise figures are available of its overall strength. Following massive recruitment over the last years, various sources estimate its strength in 2007 at 42,000.

National Security Forces

The *National Security Forces* (2005: 11,000) are the successor organisation of the Palestine Liberation Army (PLA), the PLO's military formation in the Diaspora. The *National Security Forces* recruited most of the personnel from the PLA and added local recruits gradually. Prior to the *Intifada*, the *National Security Forces* were responsible for guarding the borders of Area A and for conducting joint Israeli-Palestinian security patrols. In Gaza, the force is organised into three brigades (2005: 6,700): a northern brigade for the northern strip including Gaza City; a southern brigade for the region of Rafah and Khan Yunis, and a border brigade of approximately 1,000 troops. The border brigade in Gaza was initially set up for patrolling Gaza's border with Israel. In the West Bank, the force consists of nine battalions of around 500 troops each, which are deployed in Ramallah, Jenin, Tulkarem, Qalqilya, Nablus, Hebron and Bethlehem (overall strength West Bank in 2005: 4,500). The *National Security Forces* wear plain green or green US-style camouflage dress.

Naval Police

The *Naval Police*, the Palestinian 'proto-navy', officially protects the PNA's territorial waters and has a strength of some 1,000 men (2005). It is deployed primarily in Gaza, where it comprises about 600 men. Some additional 300 *Naval Police* are deployed in Nablus, Bethlehem and Jericho in the West Bank. Besides its naval activities, the organisation has actively participated in interrogating opposition activists and

132

collaborators. During the *Oslo* years, the mandate of the *Naval Police* also included the protection of the President of the PNA. The *Naval Police* wear different uniforms, including brown-beige US camouflage uniforms.

Military Intelligence

The *Military Intelligence* comprises some 500 to 600 plain-clothes agents (2005) who collect intelligence on the external military environment. Under Arafat, however, it acted primarily as an internal security organisation for monitoring and repressing opposition from within Fatah. The organisation has been officially integrated into the *National Security Forces* as the *Military Intelligence Department*.

Military Police

The *Military Police* was part of the *Military Intelligence* until it became a separate unit of the *National Security Forces* in 2005. The *Military Police* enforces order and discipline among the various security organisations and provides backup support to riot control and infrastructure protection. The *Military Police* has one reinforced battalion (2005: 1,400) in Gaza and one regular battalion (2005: 600) in Ramallah. The unit wears plain green or green US-style camouflage with red berets.

Military Liaison

The *Military Liaison* (2005: 100) coordinates security with Israel and is in charge of the PNA elements in the District Coordination Offices (DCO). It conducted joint Palestinian patrols with the Israel Defence Forces (IDF) until its function became obsolete with the outbreak of the second *Intifada*. Technically it is now a department of the *National Security Force*s.

Presidential Security/Force 17

The *Presidential Security*, better known as *Force 17*, is a military unit responsible for the protection of members of the PNA's political establishment, as well as for the protection of important PNA infrastructure. It has long been the 'elite unit' of the PNA. The *Presidential Security/Force 17* has a strength of some 4,500 men (2005): 2,500 troops in Gaza (three battalions, in northern and southern Gaza and Gaza City) and 2,000 in the West Bank (based in Ramallah, Nablus and Hebron). The unit wears green US-style camouflage dress with bordeaux-red berets.

General Intelligence

As the official PNA intelligence service, the *General Intelligence* is independent and under the direct command of the PNA President. In 2005, the General Intelligence was placed under the split command of the President and the Minister of the Interior for the duration of the planned reorganisation process of the PNA security sector. Its structure, organisation and leadership replicate the PLO intelligence department in exile. The organisation collects intelligence inside and outside the Palestinian Territories, counters espionage and collaboration and cooperates with foreign intelligence services. In 2007, the *General Intelligence* had an estimated strength of some 7,000 agents, divided equally between the West Bank and Gaza. Both branches also have a small paramilitary strike force.

Executive Force

The *Executive Force* consisted in summer 2007 of some estimated 6,800 members of the armed wings of Hamas and the Popular Resistance Committees (PRCs), as well as a number of members from smaller factions in Gaza. The PNA Ministry of the Interior set it up in April 2006 as an instrument for establishing law and order in the Gaza Strip. The status of the *Executive Force* has been a major source of tension between the PNA Presidency and Hamas. Talks on integrating the *Executive Force* into the *Civil Police* had not materialised by spring 2007. The *Executive Force* wear either black-blue-white camouflage or black dress.

Presidential Guard

The *Presidential Guard* was originally a military unit of some 400 men responsible for the protection of the PNA President. It had long been part of the *Presidential Security/Force 17*, but became a separate force in 2006, mainly because of US legal restrictions that prevented the US from cooperating with the *Force 17*. The *Presidential Guard* operates outside the *National Security Forces* and reports directly to the President. Its new mission includes, besides personal protection, counter-insurgency and rapid intervention tasks. In 2007, the *Presidential Guard* was set to increase its strength from some 3,500 (2006) to an estimated strength of 8,000. It also comprises a rapid deployment unit (450) in Gaza and the West Bank. The *Presidential Guard* wears green and the rapid deployment unit black dress. Its members have received training from the US, Jordan and Egypt.

Appendix B

PLC Report on the Security Situation in the Palestinian Territories and the Role of the Authorities in charge of Internal Security (May 2005)

In the Name of God, the Most Gracious, the Most Merciful

The Palestinian Legislative Council
The Tenth Term – The First Period
The Committee of Public Oversight and Human Rights

Report on the Security Situation in the Palestinian Territories and the Role of the Authorities in charge of Internal Security

Introduction

In implementation of the constitutional powers bestowed on the Palestinian Legislative Council (PLC) to hold the Executive Authority accountable; based on the role of the Committee of Public Oversight and Human Rights to exercise its oversight role; in view of the declining security situation throughout the Palestinian Territories as well as increasing incidence of killings and aggressions against citizens and public institutions, the emergence of armed militias, the rise of incidents of robbery and theft, and frequent complaints filed by citizens concerning non-implementation of judicial decisions; and in light of the conduct of some Executive officials in the Palestinian Authority, especially in the security organisations, perpetrating injustice, infringements and violations of human rights, freedoms and dignity; the Committee of Public Oversight and Human Rights hereby submits this report to your esteemed Council. The Committee beseeches the Council to take decisions to hold the Executive accountable for its responsibilities and role as well as the measures which it has taken to put an end to the deteriorating security situation. The Committee has sent letters and held meetings with the concerned authorities regarding the issues mentioned above. In particular, a meeting was held between the Committee of Public Oversight and the Committee of Interior and Security with the former Minister of the Interior.

Executive Summary

Insecurity

Palestinian society has recently witnessed a state of flagrant insecurity, resulting in the spread of several phenomena that do not conform with Palestinian society's moral and national values. These incidents are summarised as follows:

1. Spread of Killing Incidents

Over the past few years, the Israeli occupation has not only resulted in enormous losses, including the death of thousands of citizens and destruction of civilian property, but it has also affected the Palestinian social structure. As a result, incidents of killing have increased uncontrollably, creating a state of fear among Palestinians. Hence, citizens no longer feel secure or safe and the Executive has been unable to control the security situation.

Before shedding light on these incidents, it is extremely important to make a distinction between the weapon of resistance – which is not to be addressed here in any case – and the weapon of the outlawed armed militias that create the security chaos.

Regarding the increase in killings and aggressions, the Committee has received numerous complaints from Palestinian citizens. For example, a Palestinian citizen was killed in the city of Salfit two years ago. Consequently, a security turmoil and chaos erupted; members of security organisations carried weapons, abducted citizens, tortured them and opened fire on the house belonging to Dr. Shaher Ishtayyeh, Chairman of Salfit Municipality, in addition to other houses in the city. In addition, armed individuals threatened citizens and issued threatening statements and counter-statements which contributed to rising alarm and created uncontrollable chaos. All these incidents set the scene for corruption and further turmoil.

Consequently, the Committee of Public Oversight and Human Rights visited the city of Salfit to evaluate the security situation. The Committee obtained a comprehensive file about the events that took place in the city. After the Committee had examined the incidents in the city, it approached the commanders of the security organisations but received virtually no responses. Major-General Ghazi Al-Jabali, however, indicated that the police had spared no effort to enforce the law. Nevertheless, some security organisations prevented the Police from taking proper measures. While Major-General Isma'il Jaber, the Commander of National Security Forces, responded to a letter forwarded by the Palestinian Independent Commission for Citizens' Rights (PICCR), he did not respond to a similar letter by the Committee of Public Oversight.

In addition, a bloody conflict was reported to have taken place between two families in the city of Khan Younis, during which nine citizens were killed. Members of the security organisations intervened in the conflict.

In other events throughout Palestinian districts, armed individuals attacked government departments and abducted military officials and foreign nationals for several hours. On 10 February 2005, an armed group raided and took control of Gaza Prison, situated in the Al-Saraya Complex. The armed group killed three prisoners and stayed in the prison for a period of two hours. In its weekly meeting on 14 February 2005, the Committee of Public Oversight and Human Rights announced a decision to establish a joint committee between the Oversight Committee and the Committee of Interior and Security to investigate the impact of these events on the security situation and the rule of law. In addition, individuals attacked PLC offices in Gaza City and assaulted a number of PLC members. On 13 February 2005, armed individuals attacked three presenters at *Al-Quds* Voice Radio.

136

With reference to the attack on Nabil Amr, a PLC member, by unidentified individuals, the PLC issued a decision to establish an ad hoc committee to follow up on the investigation in this case. More than once did the ad hoc committee address Ahmad Qurei', Chairman of the Council of Ministers, in order to review the procedures and conclusions of the investigation. The committee received a briefing about the investigation procedures through a letter forwarded by Attorney-General Hussein Abu Assi to Dr. Hasan Abu Libdeh, then Secretary-General of the Council of Ministers. During its weekly session No. 47 on 18 October 2004, the Council of Ministers decided to appoint the former Minister of the Interior to follow up with the investigation on the attack against Mr. Amr, as well as other attacks on national characters and institutions. Consequently, the committee addressed the former Minister of the Interior on many occasions in order to view the results of the investigation. However, it has not so far received any response.

Having examined PICCR statistics, we can see the increasing incidence of murders perpetrated over the past three years: 48 were reported in 2003, 93 in 2004 and 23 in 2005.

2. Judicial Decisions Issued by Competent Courts

The Judiciary shall be a major element in establishing a society dominated by law and have its decisions implemented. Thereby the integrity of the Judiciary will be established. Otherwise, trust in judicial decisions will be lost and lawlessness will prevail.

Non-implementation of judicial decisions issued by competent courts has contributed to a further deterioration of the security situation throughout the Palestinian Territories and a state of non-confidence in the Judiciary and Palestinian Authority. In addition, it has paved the way for citizens to take the law into their own hands. The Committee of Public Oversight and Human Rights has monitored a number of complaints in this respect, including the case of Nuzha Bassoumi, a female resident of the city of Al-Bireh. Mrs. Bassoumi received two decisions from the Magistrate Court and the Court of Appeals in Ramallah to evict a tenant from her house and compel him to pay the due rent. However, the Police never executed the two decisions. On four occasions, the Committee addressed the former Minister of the Interior in this regard, but received no response. This is evidence of disdain and lack of seriousness in dealing with citizens' complaints. On 3 June 2004, the Committee also met with Wassel Al-Khatib, an official in the Palestinian Liberation Front, to hear his perspective on this case. However, the Committee concluded that Mr. Al-Khatib would not cooperate to resolve this problem.

3. Seizure of Civilian Property by Executive Officials

In light of the insecurity, the absence of the rule of law and an Executive Authority reluctant to put an end to security instability, Executive officials seized houses which they do not own, because they are members of the security organisations, related to other Executive officials or affiliated to Palestinian factions. The Committee of Public Oversight and Human Rights has monitored a number of such incidents about which complaints were made. For example, George Saleem Qare' complained that Suleiman Nayef Al-Hawarin, from Ramallah, took control of his house, claiming that he had obtained approval from the Governor of Ramallah and Al-Bireh. Additionally, Sirri Tawfiq Ibrahim filed a complaint stating that a member of the Presidential Guard seized his house in Ramallah. Abdul-Dayem Tawafsheh also complained against the officer in charge of the Criminal Investigation Department in Ramallah who threatened him after they disputed the ownership of a piece of land. (These complaints are filed with the Committee).

Due to frequent complaints sent to the Committee by citizens, the reluctance of the Executive Authority - i.e. the Ministry of the Interior - to carry out its duties and enforce law and order, because letters sent by the Committee are not responded to in most cases, and because there is a lack of seriousness to resolve citizens' complaints, the Committee deemed it necessary to meet with Hakam Bal'awi, the former Minister of the Interior, as well as a number of security officials and commanders at the Ministry of the Interior in order to gauge the real reasons which impede the enforcement of the law and public order. The following meetings were held:

Meeting with the Minister of the Interior

On 16 October 2004, the Committee of Public Oversight and Human Rights held a meeting with Hakam Bal'awi, the former Minister of the Interior, at the PLC temporary offices in Ramallah and Gaza via videoconference. Members of the Committee of Interior and Security also attended the meeting. The following issues were raised:

1. Insecurity throughout Palestinian Territories, spread of arms, and use of weapons in killings, abduction, theft and threats.
2. The security plan, measures taken by the Ministry of the Interior, and the role of internal security organisations in combating insecurity.
3. Frequent attacks on citizens as well as public characters and institutions.
4. Deterioration of the situation at crossing points and subsequent suffering of citizens.

Mr. Bal'awi affirmed his strong will to put an end to insecurity. However, capacities to achieve this end were inadequate. 'There is no security' was Mr. Bal'awi's only characterisation of the security situation. In addition, he did not refer to the measures taken by the Ministry of the Interior to address the declining security situation. Mr. Bal'awi also talked about the unclear relationship between the National Security Council and the Ministry of the Interior. Further, the Minister of the Interior did not refer to the real reasons impeding the unification of security organisations, especially those under the Ministry of the Interior. He only said that there is no liaison between security organisations. Despite his attempt to state that lack of resources had negatively impacted the security organisations, members of both Committees were not convinced that it was an adequate reason to justify the meagre performance of these agencies. With reference to crossing points and borders, Mr. Bal'awi said that these do not fall under the Ministry of the Interior's responsibility.

Describing them as 'financial petroleum wells', the Minister did not make further reference to crossing points and borders or the rent incurred from them.

In the same context, both Committees demanded that the Minister of the Interior provide it with the security plan and the Report of the Ministerial Committee on Crossing Points to which he referred in the meeting. The security plan was never provided. Consequently, the Committee of Public Oversight sent letters on 2 and 29 November 2004. No response was received.

It is worth mentioning that the Committee of Public Oversight and Human Rights sent another letter to the Chairman of the Council of Ministers on 12 December 2004, asking him to elaborate in detail on the crossing points and borders and provide the Report of the Ministerial Committee assigned to examine the reasons behind the current crisis at crossings. However, the office of the Council of Ministers did not respond.

Meeting with the Assistant Under-Secretary for Organisational, Administrative and Financial Affairs at the Ministry of the Interior

On 14 December 2004, the Committee of Public Oversight and Human Rights met with Brigadier-General Ni'man Al-Uweini, Assistant Under-Secretary for Organisational, Administrative and Financial Affairs at the Ministry of the Interior. Mr. Al-Uweini said that the Ministry of the Interior suffered from the following administrative and financial problems:

Administrative Problems

1. Tensions between the Commander of the Preventive Security Organisation and the Minister of the Interior due to promotions and transfers within the agency through administrative orders issued by the Minister without informing the Commander. In addition, a clear mechanism regulating the jurisdiction over the Preventive Security Agency in the West Bank had not been set out.
2. A number of Preventive Security officers were transferred to the Special Forces which did not fall under the jurisdiction of the Ministry of the Interior.
3. Direct intervention in the affairs of the Police without informing the Director of Police. The Minister of the Interior addressed Police officers and rank-and-file in a direct manner.
4. The Minister monopolised most administrative powers.
5. Questionable promotions which were limited to a specific group, and discrimination against persons with the same qualifications in respect of promotions.

Financial Problems

1. Uncontrolled disbursement of funds. Although a Committee of Purchases is established at the Ministry, the administrative and financial officer is not aware of financial matters. The only person authorised for disbursement is the Minister.
2. After Yasser Arafat passed away, revenues of guards at banks and financial institutions in the West Bank have been transferred to a special account under an order from the Minister of the Interior. In the past, these revenues were directly transferred to the Ministry of Finance.
3. The Ministry of the Interior received a grant to purchase 77 vehicles. However, a number of vehicles were used for personal purposes.
4. Budgets and petty cash have not been disbursed to the departments or officers since the Minister assumed his responsibilities.
5. The Minister of the Interior opened a new account under No. (630588) in the Arab Bank – Al-Bireh Branch, cancelling the authorisation of the signature of the responsible official at the Ministry.

Meeting with the Director-General of Police

In order to complete its report about the security situation throughout the Palestinian Territories, the Committee of Public Oversight and Human Rights met with Major-General Saeb Al-Ajez, the Director-General of Police. Major-General Al-Ajez highlighted the following issues:

1. The Minister of the Interior interferes with the transfers, promotions and appointments of officers without consulting with the Director-General of Police, thereby obstructing the reform plan of the Police.
2. In a meeting, the Minister of the Interior threatened a number of officers, demanding that they do not submit to orders of the Director-General of Police.
3. The Minister of the Interior's interference has caused internal tensions in the Police in the West Bank and Gaza Strip.
4. A sum of NIS 400,000 is disbursed per month for the Police instead of NIS 1,200,000 which is prescribed in the budget.
5. There is a lack of liaison between various security organisations, as well as a lack of a clear plan of preparation for the Israeli withdrawal from the Gaza Strip.
6. Since September 2004, revenues of the Police in the West Bank have not been transferred to the Ministry of Finance.

Meeting with the Head of the Preventive Security Organisation in the Gaza Strip

On 2 January 2005, the Committee of Public Oversight met with Brigadier-General Rashid Abu Shbak, the Head of the Preventive Security Organisation in the Gaza Strip, in order to complete its report about the security situation throughout the Palestinian Territories. Brigadier-General Abu Shbak emphasised the following issues:

1. The security situation throughout the Palestinian Territories is deteriorating.
2. Security organisations are reluctant to enforce law and order.
3. The Israeli occupation is a major impediment to the efficient operation of security agencies.
4. The Preventive Security Organisation has not received a sufficient budget, preventing the agency from performing its duties in an effective manner.
5. The decision related to merging the security organisations has not been implemented.
6. The Ministry of the Interior is not effective.
7. There is a lack of separation of the powers of security organisations and the nature of such powers is obscure.
8. The Preventive Security Organisation branches in the West Bank and Gaza Strip are divided. They ought to be unified into one effective agency.
9. Interventions by the Minister of the Interior in the Preventive Security organisations caused administrative confusion and disrupted the agency's operations.
10. In terms of formation and capacity, Brigadier-General Abu Shbak criticised the structure and function of the National Security Council.

Meeting with Head of Preventive Security Organisation in the West Bank

On 2 January 2005, the Committee met with Brigadier-General Ziyad Habb Al-Reeh, the Head of the Preventive Security Organisation in the West Bank, in order to complete its report about the security situation throughout the Palestinian Territories. Brigadier-General Habb Al-Reeh raised the following issues:

1. The relationship with the Ministry of the Interior needs to be rearranged.
2. Both branches of the Preventive Security Organisation in the West Bank and Gaza Strip need to be merged on a professional basis.
3. Coordination between the Preventive Security and other agencies needs to be institutionalised.
4. An inadequate amount of NIS 150,000 is disbursed to the Preventive Security Organisation per month.
5. The Preventive Security Organisation has submitted a draft law on the Preventive Security which has been forwarded to the relevant authorities as well as the Minister of the Interior.
6. Discussions have been raised with the Minister of the Interior about decisions regarding promotions, which he took without informing the Head of the Preventive Security Organisation.
7. The National Security Council does not consult with the security agencies. In addition, the Minister of the Interior does not notify the heads of security agencies of his decisions.

Conclusions

With a view to the security situation throughout the Palestinian Territories, the Committee of Public Oversight and Human Rights reaches the following conclusions:

1. Incidents of murder and armed assault rose throughout the Palestinian erritories due in part to non-enforcement of deterrent penalties by the Executive Authority. As a result, citizens will continue to take the law into their own hands and not refer to the Judiciary.
2. Violations of law and public order, as well as disrespect of judicial decisions and the principle of the rule of law have increased. In addition, security organisations have failed to take action to eliminate such incidents. Nonetheless, complaints by heads of security organisations against such a situation do not exempt them from their own responsibility for the deterioration.
3. Should the security situation continue to deteriorate, citizens will lose trust in the Palestinian Authority, thereby marginalising its role.
4. Executive officials commit murder or intervene with the Judiciary, further strengthening disrespect for the rule of law. Hence, an impartial judicial system should be established in order to review trials influenced by Executive officials in order to maintain the Judiciary's independence and integrity.
5. In spite of a decision issued to unify them and define their responsibilities, coordination between the security agencies is not only absent but conflict prevails among them.
6. Members of security organisations or persons affiliated with political forces contribute to the security chaos. Thus, the Executive Authority as well as the political organisations [*tanzim*] to which these persons are affiliated share a major responsibility for the declining security situation.
7. Sufficient legal protection is not provided to members of the security organisations. Therefore, security organisations have not been inclined to play their role in enforcing the law and fighting crime.
8. Although it is the Ministry's priority task, the Ministry of the Interior does not carry out its duties to combat the deterioration of the security situation. As such, tensions developed in the Ministry itself, thereby negatively impacting on the performance of the security organisations.
9. The Minister of the Interior has committed major violations, including interfering in the powers of the heads of security organisations without prior coordination, thereby impeding their functions and threatening the cohesion of the agencies.
10. The annual budget allocated to various security organisations is inadequate. In addition, the criteria by which items of the budget are distributed are unclear.

Recommendations

Against this background, the Committee of Public Oversight and Human Rights recommends that your esteemed Council take the following [actions]:

1. The Executive Authority should bear responsibility for the deteriorating security situation because relevant security organisations do not carry out their security duties.
2. Blame the commanders of security agencies for their unwillingness to carry out their role to put an end to the deteriorating security situation as well as demand that the newly-appointed Minister of the Interior and National Security examine this report and take the necessary decisions and measures to address existing problems.
3. Demand that the Minister of the Interior and National Security take decisions and measures to introduce substantial changes in all security organisations and put forward mechanisms and restrictions that safeguard coordination amongst them.
4. Urge the Executive Authority to complete the package of laws concerning the responsibilities and functions of the security organisations and submit them to the Council. These must be discussed as soon as possible.
5. Strengthen the role of the Judicial Authority by restructuring it as well as by creating the necessary new judicial bodies, and demand that the Executive respect and implement court decisions. As such, the Judiciary will be able to play its role independently.

Jamal Al-Shati
Head of the Committee of Public
Oversight and Human Rights

Imad Al-Falouji
Rapporteur of the Committee of Public
Oversight and Human Rights

Appendix C

PLC Report on the Unstable Security Situation in the Palestinian Authority-Controlled Territory (June 2006)

The Palestinian Legislative Council

The First Term – The Second Period
The Committee on Public Oversight, Human Rights and Public Freedoms

Report on the Unstable Security Situation
in the Palestinian Authority-Controlled Territory

Introduction

Within the scope of its work and capacity, the Public Oversight Committee examined the deteriorated internal security situation in the territory of the Palestinian Authority (PA). The Committee concludes that a state of severe insecurity and chaos dominates the PA-controlled territory: law and public order are being violated; public and private property is being attacked; members of the Palestinian Legislative Council (PLC) are being assaulted; and there is gunfire on various occasions. Also prevalent throughout the PA-controlled territory are masked individuals; robbery; citizens taking the law into their own hands; factional and family feuds; misuse of senior positions and public property; administrative and financial corruption; and various other violations. The death toll among innocent Palestinian civilians has increased sharply. Crime has also risen to an unprecedented level. According to a statement of the Palestinian Attorney-General in a hearing before the Public Oversight Committee, an average of 35 murders are reported each month in the Gaza Strip and 20 in the West Bank. In this appalling situation the Palestinian security forces do not act firmly, and some Palestinian security officers are even involved in committing atrocities. Moreover, acts of violence are common at Palestinian universities. University professors are assailed and factional and partisan disputes take place at universities. The Palestinian security headquarters and offices are also subjected to numerous attacks. In contempt of religious or national values and respect for their sanctity, medical establishments and services are also targeted.

Based on continuous monitoring of events throughout the PA-controlled territory over the past period, the Public Oversight Committee reports the following:

1. Recently, a state of insecurity and chaos has emerged. Public institutions have been repeatedly attacked. Rates of murder and crime have risen sharply within Palestinian society, resulting in major civilian casualties. Now a feeling of personal insecurity is prevalent amongst Palestinian civilians.
2. Palestinian security agencies are very reluctant to carry out their duties of preserving security and public order, as a result of the lack of political will, the culture of

144

violence dominant in Palestinian society, and the lack of discipline in the security forces.

3. From time to time, factional confrontations take place, during which faction activists open fire indiscriminately, injuring or killing innocent civilians. In essence, the lack of national unity, the absence of the rule of law, misguided factional mobilisation, the intense political orientation within Palestinian society, and the lack of freedom of expression of opinion all contribute to such large-scale violence.

4. Law and public order are violated. Instructions given by police officers regulating the traffic are not abided by. In addition, vendor stalls are installed along public roads and on sidewalks.

5. Armed gangs, who rob vehicles and trade in weapons and illegal drugs, are active in various areas under the observation of Palestinian security agencies. As they lack expedient protection, security officials are unable to take necessary measures against these gangs. Unafraid of the prospect of being brought to justice, members of armed gangs have been encouraged to perpetrate further crimes.

6. Confrontations take place between families, during which gunfire is exchanged indiscriminately. Especially in Khan Yunis, Ash Shuja'iya, Beit Hanun and Salfit, many civilians have been killed in family confrontations.

7. The rule of law and judicial authority are absent. Palestinian courts are subjected to numerous attacks. Furthermore, judges, judicial staff and members of the Public Prosecution are threatened, thereby further entrenching the aforementioned violations, perpetuating the state of security chaos, and obstructing the rule of law in Palestinian society.

8. Frequent attacks are launched against private and public institutions. As such, internet cafés were destroyed and foreign nationals and reporters abducted. All these acts flagrantly violate the values and ethics of the Palestinian people as well as the Palestinian public's will.

9. Against this background, the Public Oversight Committee believes that the causes of insecurity are:

   A. The Israeli occupation and attacks on the Palestinian people. The Israeli army kills Palestinians; destroys civilian houses; levels land; conducts extra-judicial killings of wanted civilians; imposes the closure of Palestinian territory; and restricts civilian movements. As a result, the PA has been effectively incapable of creating a state of stability or enforcing the rule of law.

   B. The harsh humanitarian situation of the Palestinian people has further promoted the state of security chaos. Following the Palestinian legislative elections and formation of the Hamas government, a severe blockade was imposed on Palestinian territory, thereby destroying the Palestinian national economy.

   C. Weak judicial authority and non-execution of judicial decisions have increased the state of security instability, as well as generated a tendency for citizens to rely on their family, tribe or party for the protection of their interests. At times, some Palestinians have committed atrocities to achieve their ends.

D. Occasional partisan and factional conflicts, accompanied by the use of arms, have instigated further confrontations.

E. Palestinian security agencies are reluctant to carry out their duties because they lack the necessary protection.

Out of a feeling of national responsibility, the Public Oversight Committee convened to look for a way out of this abnormal situation. On 6 June 2006, the Committee held a hearing session for Mr. Sa'eed Siyam, the Minister of the Interior, and heard his statements on the reasons behind the security chaos, the encroachments on governmental land, repeated murders, and the dispute between Mr. Siyam and the Director-General of Internal Security. In separate meetings, the Committee did not spare efforts to resolve the dispute between the Minister of the Interior and the Director-General of Internal Security. In addition, the Committee requested that the PA President and Chairman of the Council of Ministers resolve this dispute. As a result, the dispute was partly resolved and the operating of the Ministry of the Interior improved. Additionally, the Committee planned to hold a meeting with the Director-General of the Police and hear his statements on the current situation, the means to avoid it, and the role to be played by the police forces in enforcing the rule of law.

On 26 June 2006, a delegation from the Public Oversight Committee, comprising Dr. Faisal Abu Shahla, the Committee Chairman, Dr. Marwan Abu Ras, the Committee Rapporteur, and Mrs. Intisar Al-Wazir, Committee member, visited the Director-General of the Palestinian Police at his office. With regard to the state of insecurity, the Director-General of the Police explained the problems and obstacles impeding the work of the police: the police forces lack the necessary equipment and armaments, police stations are being destroyed and police officers have not been receiving their salaries, thereby affecting their performance. In addition, police vehicles are damaged and the police have no workshop to repair their vehicles. Furthermore, both the PA and the police fail to command the necessary respect from the general public. Some police officers are also involved in family and partisan conflicts. All of these factors have had an adverse impact upon the role and duties of the police. The Director-General of the Police also stated that he was in an embarrassing position regarding correspondence between the Minister of the Interior and Director-General of Internal Security. "In order to curb the state of security chaos", he concluded, "a strong police agency should be established."

On 8 June 2006, the Public Oversight Committee held a meeting with Ahmad Al-Mughni, the Attorney-General, to discuss the state of insecurity, financial corruption and the status of the Public Prosecution. Al-Mughni addressed high rates of crimes, death tolls, abductions, pillage and the racketeering business throughout the PA-controlled territory. In regard to financial corruption (which he addressed at a previous press conference), Al-Mughni elaborated on the financial corruption in the Public Petroleum Commission and the release of Harbi As-Sarsour, who was charged with embezzling approximately 100 million dollars. Fearing that he could escape, the Public Prosecution will appeal against the decision to release As-Sarsour. In addition, Al-Mughni addressed a number of financial corruption cases and the role of the Public

Prosecution in drawing up bills of indictment against persons involved in the embezzlement of public funds.

With respect to the state of insecurity, the Attorney-General said that the due respect of the PA and the police must be restored. Moreover, a strong and highly professional police force must be established. A judicial police force should also be established to provide protection to the Judiciary, courts and judges.

Finally, Al-Mughni addressed several other issues and answered questions raised by the Committee's delegation.

On 15 June 2006, the Public Oversight Committee held another meeting with the Attorney-General to further discuss the issues raised in the first meeting, as well as to suggest solutions to cope with the current unstable situation.

Against this backdrop, the Public Oversight Committee deems that the roots of the present predicament should be addressed and recommends the following:

1. Appreciating the formation of the National Unity Government, the Mecca Agreement, the state of national unity between Palestinian factions and forces, the Public Oversight Committee calls for further dialogue between the Palestinian factions as well as the provision of the mechanisms, controls and standards that determine the relations between them. Since disagreement between the Palestinian factions has given rise to the state of insecurity, all factional disputes must be resolved. In addition, the principle of the 'one authority' must be respected.

2. Put an end to the escalation and media statements, as well as restricting political polarisation within Palestinian society.

3. Disseminate the culture of democracy, fraternity, tolerance and freedom of the expression of opinion through the mass media, as well as organising public meetings and conventions. In addition, courses on democracy, political pluralism and the rule of law are to be included in the curricula of all educational institutions. Furthermore, the culture of favouritism and nepotism must be combated. The Committee also calls upon all Palestinian factions to avoid negative factional and intellectual mobilisation and partisan intolerance. Instead, political pluralism must be promoted.

4. Expedite the enactment of a law that regulates partisan activities.

5. Prohibit the phenomenon of individuals wearing masks within Palestinian society.

6. Cease factional and family support to any individuals who commit violations of the law.

7. Establish the rule of law, restore respect and integrity to the Judiciary and safeguard judicial independence. The Judiciary must also be established on sound grounds. In addition, the PLC must approve consolidated laws so as to regulate and invigorate the Palestinian legal system in both the West Bank and the Gaza Strip.

8. Establish a judicial police force to provide protection to the Judiciary, judges and courts, as well as executing judicial decisions.

9. Call upon the PA President to establish the High Constitutional Court in order to expedite adjudication of constitutional disputes.
10. Establish a parliamentary committee on national dialogue at the PLC. The committee should comprise the two major parliamentary blocs, other parties and the PLC Chairman to follow up on the national dialogue and present relevant results to PLC members.
11. Control arms belonging to the Palestinian factions and resistance activists and prohibit the use of arms within Palestinian society. Arms must not be used in Palestinian cities, villages and residential compounds.
12. Stipulate that personal arms must be licensed by the Ministry of the Interior, according to the law.
13. Bring any civil or military functionaries who obstruct police duties to justice.
14. Do not politicise the PA security agencies and ministries, but prevent partisan, factional or family affiliations from taking control of security agencies and ministries.
15. Oblige all security forces not to violate their powers when enforcing public security. Each security agency must be bound to its assigned duties. In addition, members of security agencies must maintain their allocated positions. If negligence is proven, the members concerned must be disciplined.
16. Rehabilitate the security agencies and provide educational courses to security officers on law, human rights and discipline. Any security officer who commits misdemeanours or violations must be dismissed from the security services.
17. The principle of rotation in senior positions must be applied in the security agencies. Heads of security agencies must not be granted tenure in their positions for a period exceeding four years and for professional reasons, extensions of tenure may be given for one year only.
18. Within a framework of a comprehensive national dialogue, the government must find proper solutions for the casualties resulting from the current state of security chaos, thereby ensuring an appropriate level of societal peace. Under PLC supervision, the High Reconciliation Committee must be reinvigorated.
19. Request the National Security Council to submit a plan for combating the state of insecurity and chaos, including the timeline necessary for its implementation.

Lastly, the Committee on Public Oversight, Human Rights and Public Freedoms beseeches all Palestinian citizens, families, factions, parties and forces to contribute to eliminating the phenomenon of insecurity within Palestinian society.

Marwan Abu Ras

Rapporteur of the Committee on
Public Oversight and Human Rights

Faisal Abu Shahla

Chairman of the Committee on
Public Oversight and Human Rights

List of Contributors

Majed Arouri is Programme Manager at the Palestinian Independent Commission for Citizens' Rights (PICCR) in Ramallah. He also worked as a reporter and editor for various Palestinian media outlets in the 1990s. He is the author of the *The Youth Revolution* (Ramallah, 1993), a study on Palestinian youths during the first *Intifada*.

Mamoun Attili is Head of the Documentation Unit at the Palestinian Independent Commission for Citizens' Rights (PICCR) in Ramallah. From 1998 until 2005, he was the PICCR Field Researcher for the Nablus area. Mamoun Attili is the author of various articles and other publications, including 'Palestinian Security Sector Governance and Legislative Oversight' (in: PASSIA-DCAF (eds.), *Palestinian Security Sector Governance: Challenges and Prospects* (Jerusalem 2006)).

Roland Friedrich is Adviser and Head of the Project 'Palestinian Territories'at DCAF. He is the author of *Security Sector Reform in the Occupied Palestinian Territories* (2004) and has written extensively on Palestinian security sector governance and reform. His research interests include the Israeli-Palestinian conflict, the Palestinian national movement, the international and domestic politics of Syria, Lebanon and Israel, the politics of Islamic and national identity, and theories of international politics.

Ghazi Ahmad Hamad is Spokesman for Ismail Haniya (Hamas), Gaza. From March 2006 until June 2007, he was Spokesman for the 10th and 11th Palestinian government. Before this, he was Editor-in-Chief of the Hamas weekly *Al-Risala*, Gaza. He was also Head of the Islamic Salvation Party, which was formed in the mid-1990s and was considered the unofficial political wing of Hamas. Ghazi Hamad was imprisoned by Israel from 1989 until 1994 and several times by the PNA throughout the 1990s.

Ahmad Hussein is a senior serving officer in the Palestinian National Authority. He chose to submit his chapter under a pseudonym.

Maen Ida'is has been Coordinator of the Public Policy and Research Unit at the Palestinian Independent Commission for Citizens' Rights (PICCR) since 2001. Before assuming his current position, he worked as Project Coordinator and Researcher with the Palestinian Society for the Protection of Human Rights and the Environment (LAW). He is the author of a series of publications, including *The Jurisdiction of the Palestinian Police* (2004), *Public Institutions and the Palestinian Executive Branch - Problems and Solutions* (2003), and *Detention in the PNA-Controlled Areas - Legality and Application* (1999).

Asem Khalil is a Researcher at the Institute of Law at Birzeit University, Ramallah. He is the author of *The Enactment of Constituent Power in the Arab World: The Palestinian Case* (2006) and *La réforme du secteur de sécurité et le rôle de la communauté internationale: le cas Palestinien* (2006).

Arnold Luethold is Senior Fellow at DCAF and Head of the Middle East and North Africa Programme. He previously worked at the Swiss Federal Department of Justice in Bern and as Representative of the International Committee of the Red Cross (ICRC) in various postings in the Middle East and in Geneva.

Mohammad Najib has been Middle East Correspondent for *Jane's Defence Weekly* since 2001. He is also Special Correspondent on Palestinian Affairs for *Le Monde* and *Knight Ridder*. Mohammad Najib has covered Palestinian issues for the last ten years and worked with a variety of international media outlets. He was Executive Director and Programme Coordinator of the *Free Voice*.